THE COLLECTED W

VOLUME VI

BIBLICAL ANTHROPOLOGY:
MAN, SIN, AND DEATH

JACK COTTRELL

THE CHRISTIAN RESTORATION ASSOCIATION

TABLE OF CONTENTS

PREFACE

This volume contains various short essays and sermons, written and preached over the years, on what the Bible teaches about human beings. This is what systematic theology calls "anthropology," from the Greek word *anthropos*, which means "man." A systematic study of this subject covers three main areas: the *nature* of human beings, the problem of *sin*, and the problem of *death*. (I hope those with feminist leanings will forgive me for sometimes using the word "man" as a synonym for "human beings" or "the human race." That is the way the Greeks sometimes used *anthropos*.)

During my thirteen years of full-time college and graduate school, I never had a course on anthropology, or the nature of man. Nevertheless, when I began my own seminary teaching, I realized the importance of this subject and soon began to offer a course called "The Doctrine of Man." I continued to teach it at regular intervals for the rest of my career. I never wrote a book with a full systematic study of the subject, however. For a condensed version of the material in my seminary course, see my book, *The Faith Once for All* (College Press, 2002), chapters 6-7, 9-11. The chapter titles are these:

- 6. The Visible Creation: The Nature of Man
- 7. The Nature of Sin
- 9. Original Sin—Or Original Grace?
- 10. Personal Sin
- 11. Human Death

The selections included in this volume are divided into four sections. First come some general pieces that I thought would make a good introduction to the rest. The opening essay is my most recent sermon (preached 9/9/2018). It is called "Who Am I?" When I wrote it for this volume, I padded it with extra details that were not part of the oral presentation. Also, I composed it here in a less formal writing style than usual, with lots of second-person ("you, your, y'all") references.

The next general item is a four-part sermon series on life, death, and resurrection. This also is one of my more recent projects. For three or four years I was invited to give an "Easter revival" at the Pleasant Ridge Church of Christ near Aurora, Indiana. This was always the four nights beginning on Easter Sunday, through Wednesday. I tried to choose themes that were appropriate for the season. The one included here was prepared especially for that one revival series. It has not been in print before.

The second main section of this book includes five items on the nature of man. They are all short essays that were written in answer to questions directed to me, usually by Facebook friends. I thought you would be interested especially in the one about free will in heaven. Most of these were published on my website (www.jackcottrell.com), and some were published in my column in *The Restoration Herald*. I apologize for a wee bit of overlap with some other things in this book.

The next main section is on the doctrine of sin. The last two items here are short pieces from my website and the *Herald* column. I especially recommend to you, though, the first four related pieces on "The Awfulness of Sin." They are a sermon series I preached in Prince Edward Island, Canada, in early August of 1997, for the Maritime Christian Fellowship (held at the Canoe Cove Christian Camp). The host group actually asked me to speak on this subject—which was the only time anyone has ever asked me specifically to speak about SIN!

The interesting thing about this event is that it took place just two months after the opening of the 8-mile-long Confederation Bridge that now links Prince Edward Island with mainland Canada in New

Brunswick. The building of this bridge was a very big deal, and one of the most exciting things to happen in northeast Canada for a long time. Up to then, the only way to reach PEI was by ferry (and earlier by steamboat). Those who invited me wanted me to tie my messages in somehow with this bridge project, which was very fresh on everyone's mind. I did that a bit in the last of the four messages. These have never been published before.

The final section here is on the subject of death. As in the second section above, the entries under this heading are mostly pieces composed in answer to Facebook questions, and have appeared on my website or in my *Herald* column. The item called "In the Face of Death" was originally published in the *Christian Standard* (8/8/1971). It is published here with the permission of Christian Standard Media.

As usual, my Scripture quotations are from either the NASB or the ESV, unless otherwise noted.

JACK COTTRELL
September 12, 2018

SECTION ONE

GENERAL STUDIES

WHO ARE YOU?

The following is a sermon I prepared and preached for the church that I serve (as part-time teaching minister), i.e., the First Church of Christ in Greendale, IN. I preached this on September 9, 2018; so it is the newest lesson (so far) to be included in this "Collected Works" series.

INTRODUCTION

This lesson is about a perennial question that most people ask themselves at one time or another, namely, "Who am I?" It may sound like a silly question, but it is really quite serious and important. Do you really know who you are? How does one decide?

Some think this is just something you can decide for yourself, according to how you *feel* about it. They think you are what you *feel* like you are; you can be whatever you want to be. The solution is to simply construct your own identity: "I identify as …." We have recently witnessed two prominent controversies stemming from this approach to self-identity. One of our U. S. senators, Elizabeth Warren from Massachusetts, has supposedly claimed to be Native American. The basis for her claim, which has been severely challenged, boils down to this (not a quotation): "My mother told me I have Native American ancestors; I feel as if I am Native American; therefore I am Native American." For another example, a former head of the NAACP, Rachel Dolezal, claimed to be black, but turns out to be almost totally of European ancestry. Why did she identify as a black woman? She is quoted as explaining it thus: "If, you know, I was asked, I would definitely say that yes I do consider myself to be black."

One area where this way of self-identifying has become rather outrageous has to do with gender. It used to be that if you were filling out a form that asked your gender, two choices were given: circle the M or the F. No longer! For example, if you want to apply to take the LSAT (Law School Admission Test), you have twelve gender choices. If you want to fill out the application to join the Facebook community these days, it is reported that you have 71—that's *seventy-one*—gender choices. One website I checked that lists possible gender identities had 48 choices under the letter A.

Another common approach to self-understanding is based on *name meanings*. This always seemed to be the case among Native Americans. One website says the Cheyenne name Hevovitastamiutsto means "whirlwind." On a simpler level, there is always Running Bear, who loved little White Dove. I guess all new parents agonize over what to name their baby. I found a website ("Mom Junction") that claims to give the meanings for 70,000 names. I know my first name, Jack, means "God is gracious," so I looked up my middle name, Warren. It said: "No data found—try another name."

If you don't trust your feelings or the name game, you can always send some saliva to one of the companies that will analyze your DNA. There are quite a few; I have seen ads from Ancestry and 23andMe. For a price (usually about $100 and up) they tell you all your main ancestral origins, e.g., one can be 8% Spanish, 17% Greek, 12% Chinese, 44% German, and 9% unknown. (Is this for real??)

How fortunate you are to be reading this, because I am going to save you some money and tell you WHO YOU ARE right now, *for free!* There is just one qualification: I cannot tell you your *individual* identity, i.e., the things that are true about you specifically and uniquely. Sorry. But I *can* tell you the identity you share with the *whole human race*, at least on some things, as well as the identity you share with all other Christians. So, unless you are an alien from Mars or somewhere, here is the answer to your question, "Who am I?"

I.   YOU ARE 100% CREATED

The first and most important element of your identity is this: you are *100% a CREATURE*, a created being. This is a quality you share with every other human being; there is no exception.

Regarding this feature, there are just two possibilities: you are either created or not, created or uncreated. Those who claim to be uncreated have just two choices for the ultimate origin of the stuff out of which their bodies are made. That stuff is either eternal, having always existed in some form or another; or it just popped into existence out of nothing purely by accident. Either way, given the existence of physical matter, how did the *living* matter that became animals spring forth from it? Purely by accident. Then we have to ask, how did *consciousness* develop within one of these animal forms? Purely by accident. So if you are not created, you have the honor of identifying as: an accidental blob of matter.

The other choice, and the one that is actually true, is that the human race was created by the almighty Creator of the entire universe. In the very beginning God created the entire universe (Genesis 1:1), then over the next span of time (Genesis 1:2-25) He made it into a comfortable home for the creature that this was all leading up to: *man* (human beings, the human race). Then when it was all ready, He said, "Let Us make man in our image." And then: "God created man in His own image" (Genesis 1:26-27). This is the foundational answer to the question, "Who am I?" – "I am a creature of God."

Some may not like this choice because they are turned off by the very word "creature." It conjures up the monsters that are a common feature in some horror movies: "The Creature from the Black Lagoon," "The Swamp Creature," "The Creature that Walks Among Us." Forget about that. Don't use the word "creature" if you think it is demeaning. Just say, "I am a created being."

Whatever term we use, many people *prefer* the non-creature answer, because if we are created beings, therefore having a personal Creator, then we have someone who has the right to tell us what to do, and to whom we must answer for our choices. And many if not most people have decided that they *do not want* somebody, especially a *divine, all-powerful* somebody, trying to tell them what to do. Therefore, to justify their own freedom to do and be whatever they *want* to do or be, they prefer to be an accidental blob of matter rather than a creature of the all-loving and gracious Creator.

The fact is, however, that the only reasonable choice, and the only truly preferable choice, is our identity as created beings. Genesis 1 tells the truth. And it is not just a *fact* that we are created beings; we should understand that it is a *wonderful, awesome, fantastic* fact that we have this identity. Also, it is extremely important to know this and to be constantly aware of it. The fact that you are a creature of God is the most important thing you can know about yourself.

- As created, we have a *Creator*; we are not here by chance or by accident.

- As created, we have a "Boss," or someone who has *absolute authority* over us, someone who does have the right to tell us what to do and to hold us accountable for it. We are not free to do whatever we want to do, including make up our own identity.

- As created, we have a *purpose* for being here, a purpose to live for, namely, to glorify our Creator-God and to live with Him forever as part of His human family.

In the heading for this section I said that we are *100%* created. What is that all about? This is about the fact that as human beings, we are made of two parts: a physical body and a spiritual soul, i.e., a body made of physical stuff and a soul made of spiritual stuff. (The latter is often called "the spirit.") To say that we are 100% created means that both parts of our being—body and soul—are created, i.e., made of stuff that at some point was created *ex nihilo*, out of nothing, by the God of the universe.

The first human being, Adam, was the fountain from which all the material from which the bodies of subsequent human beings have been made, even that of his wife, Eve (Genesis 2:21-23). Genesis 2:7 tells us where Adam's body came from: " Then the LORD God formed man of dust from the ground, and breathed into his nostrils the breath of life; and man became a living being." This shows that Adam himself was not created directly from nothing, but from "dust from the ground." But where did that dust come from? See Genesis 1:1, "In the beginning God created the heavens and the earth"! From what? From nothing! In the final analysis, the physical part of every human being has been created out of nothing by the only One who is capable of such a thing: the almighty Creator-God!

You may have heard this story, but I have to include it here anyway. God was once approached by a scientist who said, "Listen, God, we've decided we don't need you anymore. These days we can clone people, transplant organs, and do all sorts of things that used to be considered miraculous." God replied, "Don't need me, huh? How about we put your theory to the test. Why don't we have a competition to see who can make a human being, say, a male human being." The scientist agrees, so God declares they should do it like He did in the good old days when He created Adam. "Fine" says the scientist as he bends down to scoop up a handful of dirt. "Hey, wait just a minute," says God, shaking His head in disapproval. "Not so fast. You go get your own dirt."

As we have just seen, our physical part has been created out of dirt that was created out of nothing, by the only One who is capable of such a thing. Some might object to my use of the word "dirt." Our Bible translations say Adam was created from "dust from the ground." I looked up the Hebrew word translated "dust," which is *'apar*. It means "dust, loose earth or soil." When I was growing up, *dust* is what collected in the house on the furniture. If you picked up a handful off the ground, it was DIRT.

Folks, our bodies came from DIRT! But it was the good *clean* dirt that God created! It is much better to be made from God-created dirt than to be nothing more than an accidental blob of stuff.

But what about the human *soul?* Unless one believes that our soul-stuff has been around forever, or that it somehow evolved out of the physical stuff (which a few people do), then it too is the product of divine *ex nihilo* creation. Does anyone actually believe that the soul is eternal? Yes, many pagans believe that human souls have existed forever, not necessarily as individual souls, but within or as a part of some eternal spiritual deity. Somehow a piece of that deity got separated from the deity itself, and became united with some physical stuff, and voila! – a human being! Christians usually reject such a view as heretical.

Most Christians therefore view the origin of the individual soul as an act of creation, either directly or indirectly. The latter view is called traducianism (from Latin terminology involving inheritance). It is the idea that the souls of Adam and Eve were originally created from nothing, but the souls of their offspring are passed along by or inherited from their parents, just the same as the physical body is. Thus the individual soul is not directly but rather indirectly created, since it derives ultimately from Adam and Eve. This view has little or no valid support in Scripture, in my judgment.

The other view common among Christians is that the soul of each individual is directly created from nothing at the moment the body is conceived in the mother's womb. The Bible does not specifically say this, and it is difficult to wrap our minds around how this works; but I believe it is the better view. One Bible text that is usually cited as supporting this view is Hebrews 12:9, which refers to God as "the Father of spirits." This understanding of the origin of a human soul would then be analogous to the creation of angelic spirits, i.e., each one individually.

Whichever view one takes, the main point is that the soul is created and has not been around forever. The view that the soul is somehow eternal is dangerous for many reasons, but it is even more seriously false when it is based on the idea that the human soul is actually a little part of the eternal deity. Such a view says that your soul shares the divine nature of God, and makes you, in a sense, a kind of "god." Horrors!

It is difficult to believe, but this view has been held by many serious Christians, and is allegedly derived from the Bible itself! It usually comes from a false interpretation of Genesis 2:7, quoted above regarding the origin of the body from dust. The verse says, " Then the LORD God formed man of dust from the ground, and breathed into his nostrils the breath of life; and man became a living being." The man-is-god view starts with a misinterpretation of the last phrase, "a living being." Older translations often say "a living **soul**," and this is taken to be the origin of the human soul. This is a serious mistake. The word in Hebrew is *nephesh*, which can mean soul but also often means "person, individual," which would be a proper translation here. Also, the phrase, "living being," is the same phrase used in Genesis 1:20-21, 24 for the animals God was creating. It does not refer to some special nature that only human beings have. We must conclude that in Genesis 2:7 there is no reference at all to the human soul or spirit. It simply means, "Man became a living being."

The even more serious error, though, is the false interpretation of how God "breathed into his [Adam's] nostrils the breath of life." Here the word "breath" is taken to mean "spirit." Some wrongly assume that the Hebrew word used here is the word for spirit, *ruach*, which it is not. It is the word *nᵉshamah*, which often means just biological breath—as it does here (see Genesis 6:17). This phrase has nothing to do with the origin of the human spirit. But it is sometimes taken to mean that in this act God was breathing into Adam a little part of *His own Spirit*, or divine nature. Horrors!

This view has come into the Restoration Movement, beginning with Alexander Campbell, who wrote, "Lord, what is man? Thine own offspring, reared out of the dust of earth, inspired with a portion of thine own spirit." Thus there is "a divinity stirring within him" (*Millennial Harbinger*, February 1854, pp. 63-64). He says the same in his theological work, *The Christian System* (Standard Pub. reprint, n.d.). Here he says that man is "partly celestial and terrestrial—of an earthly material as to his body, but of spiritual intelligence and divine life" (pp. 12-13).

Modern Restoration Movement writers have said the same. C. C. Crawford interprets Genesis 2:7 as picturing "the Creator stooping down and placing His lips and nostrils to the inanimate form which he had created, and then expelling an infinitesimal portion of His very own essence into it" (*Survey Course in Christian Doctrine*, College Press, I:142-143). Don DeWelt repeats this view thus: "God breathed into the dead body of Adam a part of Himself or spirit .... All men share the nature of God." "The human spirit which is the likeness or image of God comes from God as a part of Himself who is Spirit" (appendix to Russell Boatman, *What the Bible Says About the End Time*, College Press, pp. 354, 358). Other Restoration writers, referring to the soul, have said things like these: "You cannot destroy the God-part!" and "Recognize the deity who is within you."

This wrong interpretation of Genesis 2:7 is *seriously false doctrine*. You are not God/deity/god, or whatever. You are *one hundred per cent created!*

II. YOU ARE 50% CREATED IN GOD'S IMAGE

The next part of your identity comes from Genesis 1:26-27, which says this: "Then God said, 'Let Us make man in Our image, according to Our likeness' .... God created man in His own image, in the image of God He created him; male and female He created them." We learn from this that we are not only created beings, but are the only created earthly beings who are made in the image of God. This means that every human being is qualitatively different from all other life on this earth. We do not have any kind of lineage that puts us on the level of animals.

But why do I say that we are only *fifty per cent* created in God's image? Because, unlike animals, we have two parts: body and spirit (soul). Though our bodies are not derived from animals, they are made of the same stuff from which animals are made. The fact that animals are not in God's image but we are, even though our bodies are similar, implies immediately that the image of God within us is not in our bodies but in our spirits.

This is important: the image of God is *not* in your body! God is Spirit (John 4:24); even more significantly, He is *uncreated, divine, eternal* Spirit, and in His pure essence does not have any kind of form or content that can be seen or examined by us. He "alone possesses immortality and dwells in unapproachable light, whom no man has seen or can see" (1 Timothy 6:16). He has no size or shape or appearance after which our bodies can be modeled. In Bible times God occasionally appeared to human beings in certain forms, including that of human beings (e.g., Genesis 19:1ff.) and will appear so to us in our final heaven, seated on a throne (Revelation 21:3-5; 22:3-5). But God has appeared in other forms (called *theophanies*) as well, such as smoke and fire and even a dove. All such appearances, including the man-shaped ones, are temporary and do not represent God's pure immortal essence. Even Jesus's human body was made after the form of human beings, not patterned after something in God.

Some people have unfortunately misunderstood this and have interpreted God as having not just the shape of a human body but as actually *existing* as a physical-type body. The Mormon religion (Latter-Day Saints) is seriously guilty of this. Their founder, Joseph Smith, said, "The Father has a body of flesh and bones as tangible as man's" (*Doctrine and Covenants*, 130:22). This is how Jesus came into existence as the *Son* of God: "The Father came down and begat him, the same as we do now," said Brigham Young, a successor of Smith (*Discourses*, I:321).

We reject such ideas as heretical. Your body is not patterned after anything in God; the image of God applies only to your soul.

So what does it mean, to say that your soul is created in God's image? It means that we are patterned after His existence and nature as a PERSON (actually, as three persons—Father, Son, and Holy Spirit). God is *personal*, and He has created us as persons, with all the mental and spiritual capacities that He has, only on a finite rather than infinite level.

This applies to our minds, to our wills, to our moral nature, to our ability to experience emotions, and to our ability to make plans and carry them out. It also means that we can exist in a community of persons with all kinds of interpersonal relationships. But most of all it means that we can have a personal relationship with God Himself! We alone, of all earthly creatures, can consciously know God and relate to Him, person-to-person! Alexander Campbell was wrong about the origin of the soul, but he was right about what the image of God means:

> ... Man, then, was a companion of his Father and Creator, capable of admiring, adoring, and enjoying God. Having made the earth for him, God was fully glorified in all his sublunary works when they made man happy, grateful, and thankful to himself. Man, then, in his natural state was not merely an animal, but an intellectual, moral, pure, and holy being. (*Christian System*, p. 13)

We affirm, then, that our identity as human beings includes the fact that God has created us in His own image. As human beings, we are indeed special and unique among all the living creatures on this earth. We reject any accusations of "speciesism," a view (similar to racism) that attacks the idea that human beings are superior to animals in any way. We can confidently affirm that we *are* superior to animals. The problem is that we so often do not live like it.

III. EVERY ONE OF US IS A SINNER

We have begun our journey of answering the question "Who am I?" with some very positive characteristics. We are creatures of God, and we are creatures who have been created in the very image of God. But now we must turn to a negative aspect of our nature, namely, the fact that we are all sinners.

Does this mean that somehow we were *created* as sinners? No! This part of our nature does not begin in Genesis 1 and 2, but in Genesis 3, where Adam and Eve introduced the reality of sin into our universe. The fact is that part of being made in God's image means that all human beings have *free will*, and at least for us in this earthly life, that means having the ability to choose between good and evil. I.e., it means we have the capacity or ability to sin. Adam and Eve used their free will to sin against God, and so have all their descendants since (Romans 3:23).

So, what percent sinners are we? I did not include a number in the heading for this section, because on this point there is a difference among human beings. In a real sense, at the time when we *begin* to be conscious of our identity as sinners, i.e., when we reach the age of accountability, at that time we can say that we are *100% sinners*. This must not be taken to mean that unsaved sinners are as evil as they can possibly be; not even those who believe in "total depravity" (which I do not) look at the "total" this way. Rather, it means that for the unsaved, sin has corrupted 100% of their being, body and soul. That is the sense in which we all were 100% sinners at one point, in our pre-Christian state. At that time both our bodies and our souls were under the power of sin.

But given the fact that God has always been ready to save sinners after they have recognized that identity, we must say that at any time in post-Fall world history, human beings have been divided into two categories. This is especially true of the New Covenant age in which we live, because on the Day of Pentecost (Acts 2) God added an aspect of salvation that was not made available before that. What I will say below applies especially to the world population since the church began.

Here then is the way it is, as far as sin and salvation are concerned: some human beings are still *100% sinners*, since they have not heard and obeyed the gospel so as to become saved; and some—those who *have* heard and obeyed the gospel—nevertheless are still *50% sinners*. What makes the difference here is again the fact that we human beings are made of two different parts, body and soul. When sin first infects our natures and takes root therein, it actually resides in both of these parts, both our body and our soul. Most Christians understand the "soul" part; we understand that the unsaved soul is spiritually dead in sin (Ephesians 2:1, 5), that the heart or inner man is "more deceitful than all else and is desperately sick"

(Jeremiah 17:9). But we have somehow missed the point that the sinner's *body* is also under the power of sin.

This latter point is something I did not understand until I did my deep study of Romans, especially of chapters 6-8, when I was writing my Romans commentary in the late 1990s. At that time I learned that when Paul is referring to the "flesh," he is indeed referring to our physical bodies; and he is saying that in some real sense, our bodies are *sinful*. The "lusts of the flesh" and the "body of sin" are literally that. (See my commentary on Romans 6-8 for more on this. Also, please note that I am not here talking about the *physical* effects of sin on the body, such as disease and death. The sinner's body is *spiritually* affected also.)

How does this affect our self-identity now? Well, if you are still an unsaved unbeliever, you are still "dead in trespasses and sins" in both body and soul. Thus you are 100% a sinner. But if you have accepted Christ as Lord and Savior and have obeyed the gospel, you are now only 50% a sinner! The reason is that the moment of conversion affects only the soul, not the body. The body is still under the power and influence of sin, and remains so until death. This did not change at conversion. This body is already dead under the power of sin and doomed to die physically. But "though the body is dead because of sin, the spirit is alive because of righteousness" (Romans 8:10), i.e., because of the righteousness of God that was applied to us in our baptism.

Now I am addressing only Christians, and will explain a bit further why you are still a 50% sinner, rather than a 100% sinner or even 100% saved. It begins in Romans 6, where Paul explains that in our Christian baptism we died with Christ, were buried with him, and were raised up to new life (vv. 1-5). The result is what is described in verse 6: "For we know that our old self was crucified with him so that the body ruled by sin might be rendered powerless so that we may no longer be enslaved to sin." This translation is from the 2017 edition of Holman's *Christian Standard Bible*, and it is the best I have seen on this verse.

What is Paul saying here? First, your "old self" was crucified with Christ. This "old self" is your SOUL only, your old sin-infected soul. When was it crucified with Christ? IN BAPTISM. See verse 3 – you were baptized *into His death*. This is the event of new birth, regeneration, new creation; this is when the Holy Spirit made you a new person and gave you a new identity. This is why you are no longer a 100% sinner, but now just a 50% sinner. The soul part of you has experienced redemption, but the body has not.

Second, the "body ruled by sin" (Greek, "body of sin") has been "rendered powerless." This is talking about the physical body. That it is described as the body "of sin" or "ruled by sin" is what I explained briefly above. This physical, sin-ridden body *did not* experience redemption in our baptism; the sin that dwells in it was not eradicated. Nor was it at that moment even set upon the road to redemption. So what did happen to it in baptism? It was "rendered powerless." This is the Greek word *katargeō*, which can mean either "to destroy" or "to render powerless." Most versions have gone the former route; thus we see it said that the body of sin has been "destroyed," or "abolished," or "done away with." This I believe to be seriously wrong; it misses the whole point. The reason, I think, that most translations have taken this view is because they do not see the "body of sin" as referring to our physical bodies, but only to our old sinful life. This is incorrect. Throughout Romans 6-8, when Paul is talking about the body or the flesh, he is referring to our physical bodies. And here he says it is "rendered powerless." This is an absolutely valid translation of the Greek word (see Hebrews 2:14, where it refers to the devil).

So, third, what does Paul mean when he says that the body of sin has been rendered powerless? He means that it can no longer rule over our spirits, and drag us down into its sinful lusts. Because of what happened in baptism, "we may no longer be enslaved to sin." This limitation of the sinful body's power over us is not the result of something that happened to our *bodies* in baptism, but the result of what happened to our *spirits*. When our spirits were regenerated in baptism, they were given new power and spiritual strength, so that rather than our bodies ruling us (we/us = our personal spirits), we (as our spirits) can rule our bodies! The body still wants to control us, but we now have the spiritual strength to suppress it. This is why Paul can insist in Romans 6:12-14 as follows: "Therefore do not let sin reign in your mortal body so that you obey its lusts, and do not go on presenting the members of your body to sin as instruments of unrighteousness; but present yourselves to God as those alive from the dead, and your members as instruments of righteousness to God. For sin shall not be master over you, for you are not under law but under grace."

The bad news, of course, is that you are still a 50% sinner. On the other hand, the good news is that you are also *50% saved!* So which 50% will dominate in your life? This sounds in a way like a "half empty or half full" question. So what is the answer? The fact that your spirit has been redeemed gives it the solid edge, because it has been renewed and reinvigorated with power. But there is more! Not only has your spirit itself been restored to its natural strength; God has also given us the gift of the *indwelling Holy Spirit* to reinforce us in our battle against our "body of sin." This is the very point of this salvation gift, and it is the new aspect of salvation that began on the Day of Pentecost.

IV. EVERY CHRISTIAN IS A SAINT

In this last section I will not be referring at all to the situation of the unsaved, 100% sinners. Here I am talking only about us who are Christians. Also, in this discussion I will be referring only to the part of our nature that is saved, namely, our spirits. When we as Christians are trying to answer the "Who am I?" question, we must remember that we are creatures — indeed, creatures made in God's image, and creatures who have sinned. But the most comforting point is this one: our real identity is not that of sinner, but that of SAINT. In the Bible, not just certain special Christians are called saints; every one of us is a saint! This is what we become in our moment of salvation. What does this mean?

The basic meaning of the Greek word for saint (*hagios*) is "holy one"; and the basic meaning of words for holiness is "sanctified, set apart from, separated from." Thus a saint is someone who has been separated from the world, from the old creation, and from his life of sin, and has begun a whole new life with a whole new identity. The thought is captured in Colossians 1:13, "For He rescued us from the domain of darkness, and transferred us to the kingdom of His beloved Son." It reminds me of the concept we hear about in television tales sometimes, where a prize witness is taken into the "witness protection" program. This involves being separated from everything in his old life, and being given a new identity. The purpose is basically to hide from dangerous foes. Becoming a saint is a lot like this. We take on a new identity in order to hide from our enemy, the devil.

To explain this further, our sainthood is defined and measured in two ways, corresponding to the two main aspects of our salvation (usually known as the "double cure"). The first part of our salvation is that God has *justified* us, which means the same as forgiveness of sins. Justification is a legal concept; it is an act of a judge when a person charged with a crime is standing before him. It is the judge's declaration of his decision in the case, which is one of two possible decisions. One such decision is to convict the defendant of the crime with words of *condemnation:* "Guilty! Ten years in prison! Take him away!" The other possible decision is this, when the judge says, "No penalty for you! You can go free!" This latter is the essence of *justification.* You will notice that the judge does not have to say, "Not guilty!" The main thing is the "No penalty for you!" This is exactly the way it is when our heavenly Judge justifies us. We stand before him *guilty*, and He knows it; but nevertheless He looks at us and declares: "No penalty for you!"

How can He do this? When God justifies us, He is forgiving our sins. To have one's sins forgiven means that you do not have to pay the penalty they deserve. It is like owing a debt and being told, "Forget about it. We're even." Here is where we can start talking about percentages again. When we are justified, having our sins forgiven, *what per cent justified or forgiven are we?* The answer is: 100% justified! One hundred per cent of our sins are forgiven. We do not owe God any of the penalty for our sins. "There is therefore now no condemnation for those who are in Christ Jesus" (Romans 8:1).

But how is this even possible, given the fact that God is a holy and righteous Lawgiver and Judge? How can He simply say, "Fuhgeddaboudit!" Whoops, I mean, "Forget about it!" The fact is that we do not have to pay our sin's penalty because Jesus has paid it in our place! When Jesus went to the cross, He was taking our place and suffering the penalty we owe. God "made Him who knew no sin [i.e., Jesus] to be sin on our behalf, so that we might become the righteousness of God in Him" (2 Corinthians 5:21). In the crucifixion transaction Jesus took on our identity, the identity of a sinner as the Father saw Him; and God the Father poured out on Him the wrath we deserve.

The reason the righteous God is able to justify us, i.e., forgive our sins, is because of *our* new identity! When our "old self" was crucified with Jesus (Romans 6:6) and we became new creatures in our baptism, we became *saints*. And this sainthood separates us from our old life and gives us a new one, a whole new identity. What is that new identity? It is the identity of Jesus Himself! Just as Jesus put on our sinner's mask when He went to the cross, He now gives us the mask of His own face! Jesus not only traded places with us; He traded *faces* with us! When God looked at Him on the cross, He saw your face, and mine. When God looks at us when we come up out of the waters of baptism, He sees the face of Jesus! Jesus put on our sin, so that we can put on His righteousness (2 Corinthians 5:21 again)! The result: we are 100% justified.

But what about the other part of the double cure, namely, the divine acts of regeneration and sanctification themselves? In addition to taking away the guilt of our sin, God's salvation takes away the *sin itself!* This recalls that moment in Christian baptism when the deadness of our pre-Christian spirit was itself put to death and buried in the waters of baptism, and we came out as a new person. This is not just a new identity, but a new actual *person*. Our nature has been brought from death to life, and our sin-sick soul is now in the process of being *healed*. Our lives are actually changing; the Holy Spirit is at work in us, purifying our wills and our deeds (Philippians 2:13). He is *sanctifying* us in another sense—not just the initial separation from our old life, but the continuing separation from the sins that so easily beset us. This is like weeding the garden, pulling up one weed (sin) at a time.

In terms of percentages, the question we can ask here is this: *How GOOD are you?* Remember, you are 100% justified. So are you also 100% sanctified? I will answer for every Christian still on this earth: NO! In this lifetime, in my judgment, no one will reach complete sanctification. Some believe it is possible, but I do not. One of the main reasons is that we are still stuck with this old sinful body until the time of our physical death (or until Jesus comes, if that happens first). From the way Paul talks about it in Romans 6-8, I conclude that even though we now have power over our bodies (rather than vice versa), we will not gain perfect control of ourselves as long as we are still in this lifetime.

So, since you are at least partially sanctified, how good *are* you? 40%? 69%? 85%? The fact is, we have no way of measuring it. Only God knows the specific number. The good thing about it is that it does not have to be a certain number for us to remain 100% forgiven. The only thing we want to be sure of is that whatever that number is, it is always getting higher and higher. We must be always growing in the grace and knowledge of our Lord Jesus (2 Peter 3:18), becoming more and more mature in our holiness (Ephesians 4:13-14). For example, let's say you began your Christian life (at your baptism) when you were 32% good. Maybe ten years later you were 53% good. And now, you might be – who knows? – 64%, or 71%, or 87% good! Only God knows. He just wants you to keep getting better.

Here is one thing we do know about that level of sanctification, though. No matter what per cent good and holy we will be when we die and leave this old body behind, at that moment when our spirits enter the heavenly throne room with God the Father and Jesus on their throne, we shall immediately become 100% good in our spirits! I take this to be the meaning of the reference to "the spirits of the righteous made perfect" in Hebrews 12:23. This is when the complete sanctification of our spirits becomes a reality.

Here is one more thing about our future identity. Our eternal identity is not finalized by our being fully sanctified at death. There is one thing yet to come, and it will happen at the second coming. When Jesus returns, our perfected spirit, which has been existing since our death in a state of bodilessness (2 Corinthians 5:1-5), will finally be clothed with a *new body*, perfectly glorified like the one the risen and ascended Christ has even now (Philippians 3:21). In that moment we will have our glorious eternal identity, in terms of salvation thus: 100% justified, which we have been since baptism; 100% holy, which was God's gift to us at death; and now 100% complete, with the addition of the glorified body. And that's who we will be for eternity!

CONCLUSION

Before we close, let's answer the question with which we began, "Who am I?" If you are a Christian, you can say—

- I am 100% created: "the creature from the mind and hand of God."
- I am 50% made in the image of God, in my spiritual nature but not my body.
- I am a sinner. This means my body is still 100% under the curse of sin.
- I am also a saint. This means my spirit is 100% saved. This means that –
- I am 100% justified (forgiven) by the blood of Christ (Romans 5:9).

- I am ?% good (sanctified) at this point, but always rising on the scale of holiness.

If you are not a Christian, you need to surrender to Jesus Christ right now, and change your identity!

A MATTER OF LIFE AND DEATH

PART ONE: THE LIVING GOD

[For most of my 49-year teaching career in Cincinnati, I taught a course called *Basic Theology*. When I began to teach it in the fall of 1967, I was putting it together "from scratch," so to speak. I was not following any existing theology textbook, but I was trying to cover most of the traditional categories of systematic theology.

In the beginning I wrestled with two ways to structure the material. One was to use the theme of "Old Creation, New Creation." I had preached a sermon a couple of years earlier with a similar title. The sermon outline was this:

I.   The Old Creation:
   A.   Created (doctrine of man);
   B.   Corrupted (doctrine of sin);
   C.   Condemned (doctrine of death).

II.   The New Creation:
   A.   Commenced (doctrine of Christology);
   B.   Continued (doctrine of the church);
   C.   Consummated (doctrine of eschatology).

The next time I preached this sermon, I had to divide it into two parts. Then the next time, I divided it into six separate sermons. (I will let you figure out where the divisions were.) In the end, this is the outline I used to construct my *Basic Theology* course. After all, "Old Creation" and "New Creation" is one way of tying all of the Bible together.

The other way I was thinking about structuring the course was around another major theme of the Bible, another set of doctrines that ties all Biblical teaching together. Indeed, it may well be even more fundamental that the creation theme. It makes sense to think that this could be the *main theme* of the essence of the Bible: *LIFE, DEATH, AND RESURRECTION.* Though I did not use this for my course outline, these concepts were prominent in it from beginning to end.

A few years ago I was asked to preach the spring 2016 Easter revival at the Pleasant Ridge Church of Christ near Aurora, Indiana. I decided there would be no better theme for an *Easter* revival than: *life, death, and resurrection!* I constructed four sermons for that purpose, and I have here written them up for publication for the first time, just to use in this volume on the Biblical teaching about the nature of human beings.]

INTRODUCTION

The created universe in which we exist is composed of several layers of reality. The bottom layer we will call the *inorganic* material which exists all around us and throughout the universe. This is the non-living layer of reality. It has no life, and was never intended to be "alive." It's not really dead either, since only things that were once alive can be "dead." Here we are simply talking about non-living stuff, such as the various minerals one learns about in science courses. Some of us will remember the early game show on radio and television (in the 1940s and 1950s) called "Twenty Questions." The panel of questioners tried to guess the identity of a selected object after being told only whether it was in the category of animal, vegetable, or mineral. Basically, if it is not animal stuff or plant stuff, it's a mineral. Animals and vegetables have life; minerals do not.

The second layer of reality is made up of *living beings*. In our universe these beings are organic, or animate, or based on carbon; or they have some other feature that serious biophysicists study and argue about. Most of us would probably say something like this: "I don't know how to define a living thing, but I know one when I see it." The main categories are the other two clues from "Twenty Question": animal and vegetable. This layer of *living things* is ensconced within its supporting mineral layer.

The third layer of reality is *spiritual*; and in this visible universe it exists in only one species of the members of the "animal" category, namely, the human race. We human beings have plenty of minerals within us; just google "mineral deficiency" and you will find that you have iron, zinc, chromium, and many others. We human beings are also *living* creatures, but in fact we are neither vegetables nor animals. We are in a category by ourselves, because we are the only kind of earthly being that possesses a *spirit* or soul. This is the seat of our personhood, and it is what enables us to relate to God, who is uncreated spirit.

Of these three layers of created reality, the one we are focusing on in this series of essays is the middle one, *living beings*. Life is such a common aspect of our world that it is easy to take it for granted. It is indeed so obvious and so all-pervasive that we forget how absolutely marvelous a phenomenon it is, which is something we want to stress here. Also, we will show how life is both absolutely strong, since it is a characteristic of God; and also how it so tragically fragile, since it is so easily lost within our earthly context. Because of the latter, we will focus on how life and death are central aspects in the whole Biblical message of sin and salvation.

In this lesson our purpose is to shed some light on the most marvelous example of life, and the source of all other life, namely, *the Living God*!

I.   YAHWEH – THE GOD OF THE BIBLE – IS *THE LIVING GOD.*

Looking at reality from another perspective, we affirm based on the Bible that among all things that exist and are real, they are composed of only two kinds of being or essence. I.e., they are either made of material stuff, or are composed of spiritual stuff (essence). Here we are focusing only on the latter, i.e., *spirit*. The Bible tells us that there are three separate spheres of living *spiritual* beings. One is the human race, which is the crowning creature of this visible universe in which our earth exists. Colossians 1:16 tells us, though, that God created *two* universes: this visible one, and an invisible one. The latter is the realm in which angels dwell, and they are the second sphere of living spiritual beings.

The final sphere of living spiritual beings is: *the Creator-God Himself!* If I were to ask you to name some attributes of God, how many would say – LIFE? Sometimes we forget that in the Bible He is often called "the *living* God." For example:

- Psalms 42:2, "My soul thirsts for God, for the living God."
- Psalms 84:2, "My heart and my flesh sing for joy to the living God."
- Matthew 16:16, Jesus is "the Christ, the Son of the living God."
- 1 Timothy 3:15, God's people today are "the church of the living God."
- Psalms 18:46, "The LORD lives, and blessed be my rock, and exalted be the God of my salvation." (Remember the song: "I will call upon the Lord....")

This fact, that God is the *living* God, is so important that God Himself used it as the basis for His most sacred promises, given in the form of an oath. Hebrews 6:17 tells us that for our assurance Yahweh often reinforced His promises with an oath: "In the same way God, desiring even more to show to the heirs of the promise the unchangeableness of His purpose, interposed with an oath." Verse 18 says that God assures us with "two unchangeable things in which it is impossible for God to lie," namely, His promise and His *oath*.

What was the nature of such an oath? In the Old Testament Scriptures one of God's most common oaths was to this effect: "I declare to you that just as sure as I am the LIVING GOD, I guarantee you that I will keep my word!" E.g., in Numbers 14:28, He says, "**As I live**, says the

LORD ...." In Deuteronomy 32:40, He says it this way: "Indeed, I lift up my hand to heaven, and say, **as I live forever** ...." So too in Ezekiel 5:11, "So **as I live,** declares the Lord God ...." And also Zephaniah 2:9, "Therefore, **as I live,** declares the LORD of hosts ...."

Men of God also swore this oath from time to time: "Just as sure as the Lord lives, I guarantee you that this is the truth...." One website cites thirty-five occurrences of such an oath in the Old Testament, as translated in the NASB. For example, in 1 Samuel 19:6, speaking of David, "Saul vowed, 'As the LORD lives, he shall not be put to death.'" In Jeremiah 4:2, the prophet says, "And you will swear, 'As the LORD lives,' in truth, in justice and in righteousness; then the nations will bless themselves in Him, and in Him they will glory.'" For others see https://bible.knowing-jesus.com/phrases/As-the-Lord-Lives.

What all of this shows is that the fact that Yahweh God is the *Living God* is the most certain of all truths.

II. WHY IS THIS IMPORTANT?

Why is it important to think of God as the Living God? What is the significance of this in our daily life and worship? What is the point in stressing the fact that God is truly alive? The main reason is this: it represents the truth of God's *unique, singular existence.* Contrary to all the so-called deities created and worshiped by fallen mankind, the God of the Bible, the God of our Lord Jesus Christ, is the one-and-only God who really, truly exists, the only One who is truly *alive!* He is the only *real* God!

How many false deities has sinful man claimed to exist? I found a book in our seminary library written by Michael Jordan [no, not *that* one!], called *Encyclopedia of Gods: Over 2500 Deities of the World* (Facts on File, 1993). And this was not meant to represent the entire list! I have read that the Hindu religion in India is reputed to have 330,000,000 deities. That's *three hundred and thirty MILLION!* But what does the Bible say?

The Bible is very clear and emphatic about this: that all these other so-called gods are *nothings* – DEAD, NON-LIVING nothings! They are made out of plain wood and stone and metal. Our God *alone* is the one, true, existing, Living God. See the following Scriptures:

Isaiah 44:6, 9-20 – [6] Thus says the LORD, the King of Israel and his Redeemer, the LORD of hosts: "I am the first and I am the last, and there is no God besides Me." …

[9] Those who fashion a graven image are all of them futile, and their precious things are of no profit; even their own witnesses fail to see or know, so that they will be put to shame. [10] Who has fashioned a god or cast an idol to no profit? [11] Behold, all his companions will be put to shame, for the craftsmen themselves are mere men. Let them all assemble themselves, let them stand up, let them tremble, let them together be put to shame.

[12] The man shapes iron into a cutting tool and does his work over the coals, fashioning it with hammers and working it with his strong arm. He also gets hungry and his strength fails; he drinks no water and becomes weary. [13] *Another* shapes wood, he extends a measuring line; he outlines it with red chalk. He works it with planes and outlines it with a compass, and makes it like the form of a man, like the beauty of man, so that it may sit in a house. [14] Surely he cuts cedars for himself, and takes a cypress or an oak and raises *it* for himself among the trees of the forest. He plants a fir, and the rain makes it grow. [15] Then it becomes *something* for a man to burn, so he takes one of them and warms himself; he also makes a fire to bake bread. He also makes a god and worships it; he makes it a graven image and falls down before it. [16] Half of it he burns in the fire; over *this* half he eats meat as he roasts a roast and is satisfied. He also warms himself and says, "Aha! I am warm, I have seen the fire." [17] But the rest of it he makes into a god, his graven image. He falls down before it and worships; he also prays to it and says, "Deliver me, for you are my god."

[18] They do not know, nor do they understand, for He has smeared over their eyes so that they cannot see and their hearts so

that they cannot comprehend. [19] No one recalls, nor is there knowledge or understanding to say, "I have burned half of it in the fire and also have baked bread over its coals. I roast meat and eat *it*. Then I make the rest of it into an abomination, I fall down before a block of wood!" [20] He feeds on ashes; a deceived heart has turned him aside. And he cannot deliver himself, nor say, "Is there not a lie in my right hand?"

Psalms 115:2-8 — [2] Why should the nations say, "Where, now, is their God?" [3] But our God is in the heavens; He does whatever He pleases. [4] Their idols are silver and gold, the work of man's hands. [5] They have mouths, but they cannot speak; they have eyes, but they cannot see; [6] they have ears, but they cannot hear; they have noses, but they cannot smell; [7] they have hands, but they cannot feel; they have feet, but they cannot walk; they cannot make a sound with their throat. [8] Those who make them will become like them, everyone who trusts in them.

Jeremiah 10:2-6, 10 — [2] Thus says the LORD, "Do not learn the way of the nations, and do not be terrified by the signs of the heavens although the nations are terrified by them; [3] for the customs of the peoples are delusion; because it is wood cut from the forest, the work of the hands of a craftsman with a cutting tool. [4] They decorate *it* with silver and with gold; they fasten it with nails and with hammers so that it will not totter. [5] Like a scarecrow in a cucumber field are they, and they cannot speak; they must be carried, because they cannot walk! Do not fear them, for they can do no harm, nor can they do any good." [6] There is none like You, O LORD; You are great, and great is Your name in might.... [10] But the LORD is the true God; He is the living God and the everlasting King.

Habakkuk 2:18-20 — [18] "What profit is the idol when its maker has carved it, or an image, a teacher of falsehood? For *its* maker trusts in his *own* handiwork when he fashions speechless idols. [19] Woe to him who says to a *piece of* wood, 'Awake!' To a mute stone, 'Arise!'

And that is *your* teacher? Behold, it is overlaid with gold and silver, and there is no breath at all inside it. [20] But the LORD is in His holy temple. Let all the earth be silent before Him."

Acts 14:12-15 — [12] And they *began* calling Barnabas, Zeus, and Paul, Hermes, because he was the chief speaker. [13] The priest of Zeus, whose *temple* was just outside the city, brought oxen and garlands to the gates, and wanted to offer sacrifice with the crowds. [14] But when the apostles Barnabas and Paul heard of it, they tore their robes and rushed out into the crowd, crying out [15] and saying, "Men, why are you doing these things? We are also men of the same nature as you, and preach the gospel to you that you should turn from these vain things to a living God, WHO MADE THE HEAVEN AND THE EARTH AND THE SEA AND ALL THAT IS IN THEM."

This last text is an example of how the Christian apostles and missionaries preached the gospel to pagans who worshiped false gods, such as Zeus and Hermes. They pleaded with them to "turn from these vain things to the LIVING GOD, who made the heaven and the earth and the sea and all that is in them." Paul later wrote to the Thessalonians (1 Thessalonians 1:9) about how glad he was that they had "turned to God from idols, to serve a living and true God."

III. WHAT DOES IT MEAN TO SAY THAT YAHWEH IS *ALIVE*?

What do we learn from reading through all the texts above? What do they tell us about the meaning and significance of Yahweh being the only true and living God? What is the difference between *life* and *non-life*? Two things stand out.

First, the *living* God is AWARE of everything that is going on, whereas the idols made by men's hands from physical materials can see and hear nothing. Psalms 115 declares that the carved idols have "eyes," but can't see; "ears," but can't hear, and so on. Habakkuk says their worshipers try talking to them ("Wake up! Get up!") but nothing happens.

But the *Living God* sees us all the time! Psalms 33:13-14 says, "The LORD looks from heaven; He sees all the sons of men; from His dwelling place He looks out on all the inhabitants of the earth." And when we pray, he hears us! See these assurances from Psalms 34:4, 6, 15, 17. "I sought the LORD, and He answered me, and delivered me from all my fears.... This poor man cried, and the LORD heard him and saved him out of all his troubles.... The eyes of the LORD are toward the righteous and His ear are open to their cry.... The righteous cry, and the LORD hears and delivers them out of all their troubles."

These texts show us that the LIVING GOD not only is *aware* of everything, but also is able to ACT and to RESPOND to what is happening around Him. In Psalms 115 again, the idols have "mouths," but cannot speak, "feet," but cannot walk. They cannot DO anything. But the Living God responds to our needs and acts on our behalf. He answers our prayers. The Living God is a DOER! As Psalms 115:3 says, "Our God is in the heavens; he does **whatever He pleases**."

IV. WHAT IS SPECIAL ABOUT GOD'S LIFE?

In the next lesson we will discuss the fact that within God's creation there are other kinds of life—angels, animals, human beings. What's special—different—about God's life? Let's start with what Jesus said to the Samaritan woman at the well: "God is *SPIRIT*"–John 4:24. He means that God is not like physical things, even physical things that are alive, such as animals. He is a *spiritual* being; His essence is *spirit*.

We are making a mistake, though, if we are trying to picture in our minds what a spiritual being such as God *looks* like. The fact is that God does not "look like" anything, since He is not a created three-dimensional being. We cannot think of God as having shape or volume, like created entities do. Nor can we think of God's spiritual essence as something that could be analyzed with scientific instruments. The defining element of spiritual essence is *personhood*, i.e., a spiritual being is a *personal* being, and a living person is a spiritual being. Thus to say that God is spirit means that he is personal. In fact, He is three persons—known to us as God the Father, God the Son, and God the Holy Spirit.

What does it mean to be a person, or personal? It starts with being self-conscious, being able to say "I AM." It is significant that God names Himself as "I AM" in Exodus 3:14. He knows Himself completely. As Paul says in 1 Corinthians 2:10, the Spirit (speaking of the Holy Spirit) "searches everything, even the depths of God." Another aspect of personhood is rationality, or having the intellectual abilities that we associate with a mind. In this respect God has infinite rational powers. This is more than omniscience, which means simply that He *knows* all things. He also has perfect and absolute logical and analytical abilities. A third marker of personhood is what we call "the will," as in *free will*. God weighs alternatives and makes decisions, then He accomplishes what He has willed. Also, personhood includes the ability to experience feelings and emotions. This is definitely true of God, contrary to a common misunderstanding of God's nature. Most of the things that God does in His interaction with human beings are the result of specific divine emotions such as love, mercy, compassion, grief, hatred, and wrath.

This leads me to mention one other aspect of personhood, namely, the ability to interact with, communicate with, and fellowship with other persons. This is one reason why God's *trinitarian* or three-person identity is so appropriate. Before He created, if He were only one person, there would have been no way to express His personhood, so to speak. But with three divine persons, there was always perfect personal interaction and fellowship. Also, His personhood explains why God would create the kind of worlds (visible and invisible, Colossians 1:16) that He did, i.e., worlds populated by other personal beings (angels and mankind) with whom He could interact.

All of these things are true of God because He is the *Living* God, whose essence is spiritual and therefore personal. But there must be something else that is special about God as a spiritual and personal being, because angels are also living, spiritual, personal beings; and so are human beings in their inner being or spirit. So what makes God different from these created spiritual beings?

The bottom line is that God is the only being, the only aspect of reality, that is *uncreated*, and the fact that He is uncreated makes Him infinite in every way. I.e., He is not limited by anything outside Himself. He is not limited in any of His attributes. This is why we speak of His omnipotence, and omnipresence, and omniscience. The prefix *omni-* comes from the Latin word for "all," *omnis*. That God is omnipotent, for example, means that He has ALL power, i.e., His power is unlimited or infinite.

The aspect of God's infinity that is closely associated with His identity as the Living God, and the one which I will stress here, is the fact that He is ETERNAL. There may be other ways to think of God as eternal, but the point here is that, since He is not a created being, in terms of past and future He has always existed and always will exist. He had no beginning, and will have no end. God has no birthday. He "alone has immortality" (1 Timothy 6:16). He is "the great I AM" (see Exodus 3:14). He has "life in Himself" (John 5:26). Revelation 4:9-10 depicts a scene in the angelic throne-room of heaven, where angelic beings constantly "worship Him who lives forever and ever."

That our God is the *Living God* means that He is the *Eternal Spirit*.

CONCLUSION

If you want to really see the difference between the one true Living God and all the so-called deities created by the minds of men, read 1 Kings 18:23ff. This is the account of the "contest" between the prophet Elijah and the Israelite prophets of the false god Baal. The sad thing is that so many of the Israelites were followers of this false deity—enough to support 450 such prophets.

Elijah is the one who issued the challenge to these false prophets: let's each build an altar and place an ox upon it, then we will each pray to our deity, and whoever answers, "He is God" (v. 24). The Baal worshipers agreed. They built their altar and laid the carcass of an ox on it, then humiliated themselves with excruciating pleading to their nothing-deity for hours—while Elijah mocked them. "But there was no voice, no one answered, and no one paid attention" (v. 29).

You know what happened next, when Elijah built his altar and laid an ox on it, then dug a trench around it all and poured so much water over it that the trench was filled with the water. Then Elijah prayed this simple prayer: "O LORD, the God of Abraham, Isaac and Israel, today let it be known that You are God in Israel and that I am Your servant and I have done all these things at Your word. Answer me, O LORD, answer me, that this people may know that You, O LORD, are God, and that You have turned their heart back again" (vv. 36-37). Then Yahweh sent the fire that consumed the ox, the wood, the altar stones, the dust around it, and the water from the trench.

The people's response? They fell on their faces and cried out, "Yahweh—He is God! Yahweh—He is God!" And so should we! Yahweh, now known as the Trinity of Father, Son, and Holy Spirit—He alone is the God of Israel, the God of our Lord Jesus Christ, the God of the Bible. He is the *LIVING GOD.*

A MATTER OF LIFE AND DEATH

PART TWO: THE LIVING CREATION

INTRODUCTION

The thing about life is just that – it's not a *thing*. Living things don't have a little block of "life," or a little strand or puddle or patch of "life." LIFE is a *way* of existing. It is an attribute or characteristic of some of the "stuff" that exists. "Stuff" is either ALIVE or NOT ALIVE.

I don't mean to be irreverent or impious when I say this, but we must realize that GOD truly *exists* as a divine *being*, and His existence involves "divine stuff." This is what He is composed of. And one of the main characteristics of His essence is **LIFE**. God LIVES. He is ALIVE. He is the LIVING GOD, as we explained in the previous lesson.

But God is not the only being that exists—and this is God's choice. He chose to *create* "stuff" – other stuff that exists in addition to Himself. However, this created stuff is in a totally different category. It is totally separate from God, and different from God. Different how? Like this: God is absolutely uncreated. He is eternally existing, being alive by His very nature, or as Jesus said, having life in Himself (John 5:26). But He is the only uncreated Being. Everything besides God that exists was brought into existence and began to exist. It was brought into existence NOT out of other stuff that was already there; rather, it was created *ex nihilo*, out of nothing. But it is now *real stuff*.

Now here's the deal: God made *two kinds* of created stuff. I'm not talking simply about the two created *universes* of Colossians 1:16. Rather, there are two *KINDS* of created stuff, whether in the visible or invisible universe. Those two kinds are these: **LIVING** stuff, and **NON-LIVING** stuff. That's right! Some of the stuff God created has the attribute or characteristic of LIFE. It is, by created nature, *living stuff*: it is alive; it has *life* in it. I cannot begin to tell you how *wonderful* – full of wonder – this work of God is! To create *anything* out of nothing is in itself something only God can do, and that is unbelievably marvelous. But to create *living* stuff – out of nothing – is one of the greatest accomplishments of the omnipotent power of the living God!!!

Let me sum up what I have said so far: The Living God has created two whole universes (Colossians 1:16), and these created universes are filled with *living beings*. In these universes we can identify and distinguish *three main kinds* of created life, three categories of living beings, which I will now explain.

I.   ANGELIC LIFE

God created *two* universes (that we know of!), according to Colossians 1:16. Here Paul is speaking about Jesus, and he says this: "For by Him all things were created, *both* in the heavens and on earth, visible and invisible." What is this *visible* universe? That's us! We will get to that one shortly, but for now we are focusing on the *invisible* universe, which is the world of ANGELS. Angels can appear among us here in our world; but they have their own universe, their own natural environment, their own dimension of reality. That's where they live naturally. Theirs is a *created* dimension, just as ours is. Angels have their own history, including a time when some fell into sin (2 Peter 2:4). As a result of this fall, there are two kinds of angelic beings: ANGELS and DEMONS. Satan himself is one of the fallen angels, now called demons. He was probably an archangel (chief angel) before the fall, and now he is the chief demon who exercises authority over all the other evil spirits.

All angels (unfallen and fallen) are *living beings*: made out of living stuff. We cannot see angels; we cannot touch and examine the stuff they are made of, because it is *spiritual*. I.e., angels are *spirits*, i.e., personal beings, and thus we conclude that they are made in God's image. That they are spirits is affirmed in the Bible. As Hebrews 1:14 says, "Are they not all ministering spirits, sent out to render service for the sake of those who will inherit salvation?" Demons also are often called spirits, but they are described as *evil* spirits. Luke 7:21 says of Jesus that "He cured many people of diseases and afflictions and evil spirits."

It is not specifically stated in the Bible that angels are made in the image of God, but this is the most reasonable conclusion based on what the Bible says about their activities. This also makes it clear that they are *persons*, with personal characteristics such as intellectual powers and free will and an interpersonal relationship with God.

Do angels have bodies? Actually, they *are* bodies; it is their very bodies that are made of spiritual stuff. As far as we know they are not dual creatures like us human beings, who have both physical bodies and spiritual souls, the latter being the center of our personhood. The angelic beings are not designed to inhabit our visible, material universe; that's why their bodies are different. They are not physical, but *spiritual* in some sense of that word. They are real beings, made of spiritual stuff, which is by definition *living* stuff. We don't know what their universe itself is "made of."

Angelic life is a marvel and a wonder, but it is not on the level of God's divine life. Angels are not absolute and are not independent of God. They are under His authority. As created beings, they are finite and capable of non-existence. This is true for Satan and his demons, just as it is true for all angelic beings. We should never think of Satan as a semi-divine kind of being who is somehow on a level with God, or nearly so.

We are now ready to turn from discussing angelic life to explaining the life that exists in the visible universe, the one in which we "live and move and having our being" in a physical sense.

II. PHYSICAL LIFE

Here we are reflecting on the second kind of life God created, namely, the physical life that exists on this earth. Our focus is on the first two kinds of existing realities that formed the scope of possible answers on the old "Twenty Questions" game: the *animal* and *vegetable* options. The *mineral* stuff in our universe is amazing, but that is not what we are interested in here. Animals and plants are the main categories of *living* matter on our planet, that is what we are focusing on in this lesson.

Our visible universe has many aspects that are mind-blowing, beginning with its *size*. Recent estimates put the diameter of our universe at about 91 billion light-years, with each light-year being six trillion miles. (In case you are wondering, the total number of miles is 546 followed by 21 zeroes.) Within this space are possibly two trillion galaxies of stars in our observable universe, according to the latest speculations. According to Wikipedia, "galaxies range in size from *dwarfs* with just a few hundred million (10^8) stars to *giants* with one hundred *trillion* (10^{14}) stars." And those numbers are the number of stars in *each galaxy*.

In addition to size, another totally awesome aspect of our universe is it *composition*. Every bit of its physical material is made of atoms, which are made of smaller particles; these atoms combine into molecules to form at least 118 kinds of stuff ("elements"), which are all different. And these combine into a nearly-infinite variety of created things. In the words of a recent song, "What a mighty God we serve," who can create such a universe!

But despite the universe's size and its great variety of stuff, the only LIFE in it (that we *know* of) exists on this little speck we call "Earth." And the very existence of this *life* is the most mind-blowing thing of all. What can we say about it?

A. The ABUNDANCE of Earthly Life

The first thing we can notice is how *abundant* our earthly life is. On our planet, living things are literally *everywhere!* Here are some examples that I found, looking in several places:

- "Storm clouds are full of live bacteria. Hailstones are brimming with microscopic life." (ScienceNordic.com)
- Headline: "Fountains of life found at the bottom of the Dead Sea" – small microbes and bacteria. (ScientificAmerican.com)
- Miles below the surface of the Earth: Prehistoric rocks unearthed from a gas exploration well nearly two miles below Earth's surface were found to be teeming with bacteria, which feed on rock. Tiny worms such as nematodes and flatworms are also there, feeding on the bacteria. (Smithsonian.com)
- Algae have been found living inside Arctic ice. Other forms of life live beneath the ice sheets of Antarctica.
- One-cell living organisms including bacteria have been found in core samples from drilling into the ocean floor off the coast of Newfoundland at a depth of over 5,000 feet, where the temperature is estimated to be 140-212° F. (New York Times, 5/27/2008)
- In deep caves miles below Earth's surface much life exists, including many kinds of small fish. (Planet Earth TV series: "Caves.")
- Deserts teem with life. See Disney's 1953 film, "The Living Desert." In late winter 2016, a news program showed pictures of a "superbloom" of wildflowers in DEATH VALLEY.

Such data as the above lead scientists to conclude that there is a greater variety of life in many more inhospitable places than anyone has imagined. A "living thing," by the way, is anything (a) composed of cells, (b) requiring food and water, and (c) having a life cycle.

B. The VARIETIES of Living Things

We also marvel at the great variety of earthly life. Some of the lesser forms of life are mostly unknown by most of us since they are so small. They are the kinds of wiggly things seen in pond water under a microscope. They have names like the monera life group, which includes bacteria; and the protista group, which contains amoeba and algae. Another life group that we do see more often is fungi, which includes molds and mushrooms.

What we are most familiar with, though, are plant life and animal life. On the third day of creation, after God had separated the waters from the dry land, He caused the dry land to be filled with plants and trees of all kinds. "Then God said, 'Let the earth sprout vegetation, plants yielding seed, *and* fruit trees on the earth bearing fruit after their kind with seed in them'; and it was so. The earth brought forth vegetation, plants yielding seed after their kind, and trees bearing fruit with seed in them, after their kind; and God saw that it was good" (Genesis 1:11-12). Over 390,000 species of plant life have been identified.

On the fifth and sixth days of creation God turned His attention to creating animal life (Genesis 1:20-25). On Day Five He filled the water and the air with sea creatures and birds: "Then God said, 'Let the waters teem with swarms of living creatures, and let birds fly above the earth in the open expanse of the heavens'" (v. 20). The first part of Day Six was devoted to the creation of land animals: "Then God said, 'Let the earth bring forth living creatures after their kind: cattle and creeping things and beasts of the earth after their kind'; and it was so" (v. 24). Between 1,500,000 and 2,000,000 species of animals have been formally described, and the scientific estimates of the number of species that actually exist range from 2,000,000 to 2,000,000,000.

How are animals different from plants? There are three main differences. Animals can move about, while most plants are rooted to a host, usually the earth itself. Also, animals cannot make their own food, while most plant life can. The way plants do this is a marvel of creation. As one web site sums it up, "*Plants* turn water and air into food. Water from the ground is sucked up by the roots. Carbon dioxide from the air is breathed in by the leaves. Energy from the sun is collected by the leaves. The energy is used to turn the water and carbon dioxide into food. The waste from making *plant* food is oxygen" (www.growingchefs.ca/how-plants-eat). Another way animals and plants differ is that animal life has a sense of consciousness, while plants do not. (Some disagree with that last point, arguing that there is valid evidence that plants have consciousness.)

C. The IMPORTANCE of Physical Life.

The earth is stuffed full of physical life. So what? Why is that so important? Why should Christians be so excited about it? Here are several good reasons.

First, the very **EXISTENCE** of living stuff is evidence of the existence of the Living Creator. Apart from God and creation, there is no plausible explanation for how life began. Living stuff is so *different* from most stuff in the universe. Its very *existence* is a mystery that unbelievers cannot explain. Those who deny the existence of the Creator-God have no choice but to believe that living beings just spontaneously, by chance, popped into existence uncaused, via some evolutionary process for which there is absolutely no evidence or explanation.

Let me say that again: Apart from GOD, and from the fact of creation, there is NO plausible explanation for how life began. Evolution CANNOT explain it. Evolutionists admit (this is a quote): "The leap from nonlife to life is the greatest gap in scientific hypotheses of Earth's early history." Another quote: "The origin of life. If there is a more controversial (or complex) scientific problem I have yet to encounter it." (The latter is from a website called "The Advanced Apes," 4/18/13.)

Nevertheless, unbelieving scientists are desperately trying to discover a way to explain how life began as a purely natural event, JUST SO they do not have to allow God into the picture. In 2005 Harvard University launched a project, "Origins of Life in the Universe Initiative." One of the professors said, "My expectation is that we will be able to reduce this to a very simple series of logical events that could have taken place with no divine intervention." Nothing yet!

However, in 2011 John Horgan, an evolutionist writer for *Scientific American*, wrote an article: "Pssst! Don't Tell the Creationists, but

Scientists Don't Have a Clue How Life Began." Another scientist, Robert Hazen, says that at best we can say the origin of life was an *infinitely improbable accident* that can never be duplicated. (I learned this and other data above by scanning the website of the Apologetics Press [apologeticspress.org].)

The bottom line is this: the very *existence* of living physical stuff is proof of creation.

The second thing about the presence of physical life on Earth that makes it important is its **UNIQUENESS**. We have absolutely no reliable evidence of living matter existing anywhere else in the universe. This is consistent with Genesis 1, and with the Bible's implication that the Earth is the unique center of God's attention and concern.

Occasionally our media will publish some spacecraft's picture of the surface of the moon, or Mars, or of an asteroid somewhere. We have become used to the fact that there is nothing in such pictures but *dirt* and *rocks*. The contrast with the greenery of most of the land surfaces of our earth is amazing! The implications of this are a main reason why unbelieving science is so desperate to find some evidence of life anywhere else in the universe. They think this would show that life does not have to be created, that it is just bound to pop up accidently in many places in such a vast universe. Estimates as to the number of planets that could possible support life range from the billions to the trillions. But – nothing yet!

The **COMPLEXITY** of physical living stuff is one more reason why all the physical life on this earth is important. This complexity is perhaps the most compelling proof that our whole system was designed and created by an infinitely intelligent and powerful Creator. This is the focus of the "Intelligent Design" movement, which is a crucial aspect of Christian apologetics today.

For centuries, philosophers and scientists have recognized that specific things in the universe display evidence of having been DESIGNED for specific purposes, in the world of living things especially. Popular examples are animal instincts and animal body parts, especially the amazing structure of the eye. Such data formed the basis for the teleological argument for God's existence, as found, for example, in the writings of Christian apologist William Paley (d. 1805). Evolutionists have worked *very hard* to give some other explanation for this kind of thing. This was Darwin's main motive for developing his theory of evolution—to undermine the influence of Paley and others who wanted to use the complexity of living things as proof of God's existence.

Then around 1938 something was invented that ultimately led to *undeniable proof* that living stuff is the product of what is called INTELLIGENT DESIGN: the *electron microscope*. This instrument has allowed us to magnify the interior of a *living* cell *millions* of times its natural size – and the results are *phenomenal!* What you see going on inside a single living cell shows that it was designed and put together with such amazing efficiency and intricate complexity that it COULD NOT have developed gradually, by accident. What you see is actually a miniature version of an entire modern factory.

This has led to the development of a new kind of apologetics, called *intelligent design*. Even former atheists are being converted, one of the most famous being Antony Flew, who became a theist in 2007. Though he used to be an atheist, he was convinced of the existence of God by the evidence for intelligent design. He said, "The only satisfactory explanation for the origin of … life as we see on earth is an infinitely intelligent mind."

We are talking here about the stuff YOU and I are made of: physical life! Living cells! This is one of the greatest wonders our mind can grasp!

But this is still just *one* of the things that make the physical life on earth so amazing and so wonderful. As the recent song says, "The *wonder* of it all!" Our living planet fills us with awe and worship for our Creator. All of this – the very *existence* of physical LIFE, and its *uniqueness*, and its *variety*, and its *complexity*, and its *beauty* – should fill us with wonder and awe. Such LIFE is awesome! Amazing! Astonishing! Eye-popping! Breath-taking! Mind-boggling! Absolutely overwhelming!

But such admiration and awe must not be directed simply toward this awesome stuff called LIFE, but should more appropriately be directed toward its CREATOR! When we contemplate physical earthly life, our hearts should be filled with reverence and awe and *worship* toward the Creator-God who is so intelligent and powerful that He can even think up all of these magnificent things, and then can bring them into existence out of nothing! He has made not just *stuff*, but *living* stuff!

But there's more. *Created* life is of three kinds. So far we have seen only two: angelic life, and physical earthly life. These are marvelous indeed! But the third kind of created life is even further up the scale of wonder. We are ready to discuss that.

III. HUMAN LIFE

The third and most spectacular kind of created life is *human life*, the existence of the human race. How can human life be described? In the first place, it is **unique**, when compared with all the rest. How are we different? Do we not have *physical bodies*, like animals? Yes. Do we not have *personal spirits*, like angels? Yes. But the thing is this: Only human beings are a *combination* of physical (animal) life and spiritual (personal) life. Nothing else in either universe is like us! (Animals have no spirits; angels have no physical bodies.)

Human life is not only unique; it is also **sacred**. It is the only kind of life that is protected by God's own laws, e.g., the sixth commandment: "You shall not murder" (Exodus 20:13). But even before the giving of the ten commandments, God had already made it clear that human life is unique and under His protection. Just after Noah's flood, in Genesis 9:3-6, God told Noah's family that they could eat any kind of plant and animal life; but they were absolutely not allowed to take the life of another human being: "Whoever sheds man's blood, by man his blood shall be shed, for in the image of God He made man" (v. 6).

These commands show how special human life is. They protect human life only, not animal life. There is a qualitative gulf between animal and human life. Albert Schweitzer's "reverence for life" philosophy is WRONG, since he made no such distinction. He preached reverence for the life of even ants and bacteria. But human life is special and sacred – even in the womb.

Human life is also *God-like*. Note: we are NOT GOD, not divine – never! But we are LIKE God, because we are made in the image of God, for the purpose of fellowship and communion with Him. We saw this in the quotation from Genesis 9 above, and God announced this fact at the very time He was creating Adam and Eve: "Let Us make man in Our image, according to OUR likeness" (Genesis 1:26).

Why are WE like God, while eagles, ants, lions, and orangutans are not? Because we are *persons* like God, which is the result of our being *spiritual* and not just physical. We have the spiritual and intellectual and personal capabilities of God, though they be on a finite level. We can reason and feel and plan and decide and act and communicate in ways patterned after God Himself!

Why has God made us thus? Just so we as persons may have fellowship and communion with Him, the three persons of the Trinity! This is why human life was created in the first place: for eternal fellowship with God. But for this fellowship with God to be *meaningful*, it must be *freely chosen*. What does God want from us most of all? *Love!* We know this because Jesus said the most important commandment is, "You shall love the Lord your God with all your heart, and with all your soul, and with all your mind. This is the great and foremost commandment" (Matthew 22:37-38).

But for this love to truly be *love*, it must be something we do because we *want* to do it from our hearts. It cannot be something robotic, something we have been programed to display through certain outward actions. No. If love is not something we choose, then it is not real love and affection. This means – at its very center – that human life embodies and is built around *free will*.

This leads us to a fourth aspect of human life, namely, that it is **risky**. I am not saying this is the case from our own perspective, but from *God's* perspective. Why is this so? Because when God decided to make us in His own image, this means that He gave us the gift of *free will.*

After all the superlatives I have already used above about angelic life and physical earthly life, my next statement may sound strange, but here it is: Free will is the **most remarkable** thing God has created. At least within the realm of this earthly creation (and maybe all creation), when God created *human life*, with its God-like ability called free will, this was at the top of the charts, wonder-wise.

Free will in a sense is the ability to *create* – at least, to create *events*. I.e., we cannot create stuff out of nothing; only God can do that. But we can bring other things into existence that would not have existed apart from our free-will choice. Every time we do something we have chosen to do, we have created a situation or a relationship or a solution to some problem, for example. But most significantly, free will is the ability to *bind ourselves* in a love-relationship with the Almighty Creator! We have the capacity for choosing to love God forever! This is remarkable indeed!

Because of its potential for love, free will is indeed a wonderful gift; but at the same time it is the most **risky** thing God has created, because it opens the door to sin. If free will is truly free, then it must include the ability not only to choose to *love* God, but also the ability to choose to *reject* Him. Why do we call this a RISK on God's part? Because God knew, before He made the decision to create free-will beings, that they would be able to use this free will to sin against Him rather than to love Him. And He knew, before He made the decision to create free-will beings who could sin, that He would have to do everything He could do in order to SAVE them from their sin if that was their choice. His love would demand it.

And most of all, He knew, before He made the decision to create potential sinners who would need salvation, that the only way He could save such sinful creatures would be to become a human being, and identify himself with sinners, and suffer the penalty for their sins in their place! I.e., He would have to become Jesus of Nazareth, and take upon Himself the infinite suffering equivalent to eternity in hell for the whole human race, in order to allow sinners to choose salvation.

Was God willing to take this risk? YES – and the rest is history!

CONCLUSION

Of all the majesty and glory and grandeur and splendor that have been manifested in the creation of LIFE – of LIVING THINGS, nothing comes close to the importance and magnitude of *your personal free-will choice* to say to God from your heart right now, **I LOVE YOU, GOD!** — and to act upon that love first by obeying the gospel *now* if you have not already done so, and then to obey God's laws from your heart (Romans 6:17) for the rest of your life.

A MATTER OF LIFE AND DEATH

PART THREE: THE PROBLEM OF DEATH

INTRODUCTION

So far in this series of lessons on life and death, the key word has been LIFE. God is the *Living God*, the one who has life in Himself and is the Creator of life. The *living creatures* God brought into existence fall into three categories: (1) Angelic beings with *angelic* life, which is personal spiritual life. (2) Earthly beings with *plant* life and *animal* life, which constitute earthly physical life. And finally, (3) *human* beings as combined spiritual and physical life.

In the beginning God pronounced this living universe "very good" (Genesis 1:31). But now, everywhere we look today, we see DEATH! When we read our history books and newspapers, when we watch news reports, the key word seems to be DEATH! History is filled with wars and atrocities of all kinds: genocide, the holocaust, countless Christian martyrs, numerous mass murderers such as Hitler, Stalin, Pol Pot, Mao Tse Tung; death by torture. Our biggest news items are about death: natural disasters: earthquakes, tsunamis, floods, mass shootings. We have been faced with the Boko Haram group in Nigeria, ISIS beheadings and suicide bombings in the Middle East. We read about school shootings, parents murdering their own children, and other such atrocities.

We seem to be living in a culture of death: death by neglect, death by cancer and heart attacks, death by drug overdoses, death by drive-by gang shootings, death by child abuse, death by DUI accidents, and tens of millions of abortions worldwide every year. DEATH! DEATH! DEATH! What has happened to our "very good" world? It seems to be upside down!

In this lesson we will be looking at what the Bible says about this brutal enemy, *death*.

I. KINDS OF DEATH

Our main focus here will be on human death, but we will begin with some comments on death in other spheres of life.

First, what about the invisible universe of angels? Is there such a thing as death among angels? In the Bible we are not told enough about the angelic world to know for sure how death affects it. As far as we know, angels were created individually and were intended to live forever as God's servants. The name "angel" means "messenger," indicating that they would be carrying out God's orders in some way.

Second Peter 2:4 speaks of the "angels who sinned." We deduce from this that each angel was created with free will, since the ability to commit sins presupposes free will. Among the angels who sinned was the one we know as Satan; he was probably an archangel ("chief angel") and assumed the leadership of the others who sinned. Angels who sinned are now fallen angels, called demons and evil spirits in the New Testament. They seem to have had no system or opportunity for redemption.

Is there any sense in which these angels "die," or experience death? I am not aware of any Biblical text that refers to their sinful condition as a state of spiritual death. But human sinners are spoken of as being spiritually dead (see below), so we can speculate that the same applies to the angels who sinned. Since they do not have physical bodies, we can confidently say that they do not suffer physical death. Whether there is something analogous to that we do not know. What we do know is that the angels who sinned are lost forever in eternal punishment, described as "the eternal fire prepared for the devil and his angels" (Matthew 25:41,

46). This "lake of fire" is called the "second death" (Revelation 20:14), and it is stated specifically that Satan and his followers (which would include all the demons) will spend eternity there (Matthew 25:41; Revelation 20:10). Thus, at least in this last sense, the fallen angels seem to fall under the rule of Romans 6:23 – "The wages of sin is death" – especially eternal death in the lake of fire.

What about death in the non-human living species on earth? Many assume that ALL death, even the death of animals, is the result of Adam's sin. They think that if there had been no human sin, there would be no death among animals. I seriously disagree with this assumption. I believe that when the Bible says that the wages of sin is death, it is referring only to the human race. "The soul who sins will die" (Ezekiel 18:4). There is no sense in which any animals were involved in the first sin that brought the curse of death upon the world. Some may say that animals are a part of the world that was put under the curse to punish human beings, and somehow their death contributes to human suffering while in this earthly life. I see no rationality to this kind of thinking, nor is it Biblical.

Thus I would say that the death of plants and animals is natural, and is intended by the Creator to be a benefit for human beings. The death of plants is clearly intended, since plants were meant to be the basic food for humans and animals. Genesis 1:29-30 says, "Then God said, 'Behold, I have given you every plant yielding seed that is on the surface of all the earth, and every tree which has fruit yielding seed; it shall be food for you; and to every beast of the earth and to every bird of the sky and to every thing that moves on the earth which has life, *I have given* every green plant for food'; and it was so." Also, the very process of reproduction among many plants requires that the seeds must die. Jesus said in John 12:24, "Truly, truly, I say to you, unless a grain of wheat falls into the earth and dies, it remains alone; but if it dies, it bears much fruit." See 1 Corinthians 15:36.

So we know that plant death is part of God's creation purpose and is not a part of the curse. But what about animal death? First of all, there is no **specific** reference anywhere in Scripture that specifically says that animal death is natural. We do have, however, the reference in Genesis 1:22, which says that God specifically spoke to the birds and sea creatures thus: "Be fruitful and multiply, and fill the waters in the seas, and let birds multiply on the earth." We can assume that the same was intended for the land animals. My thought is that if the natural processes of reproduction were intended to continue among all these animals without some kind of natural death processes, the seas and the land would ultimately become completely filled up and overrun with animals. E.g., the fish known as the common carp lays c. 300,000 eggs in one spawn, and can spawn several times per year, thus producing as many as a million little carp in one year. If they all lived and continued to spawn at that same rate, how long would it take to fill the oceans completely with just carp?

After the Fall in Genesis 3, the first implied death of an animal is the statement in Genesis 3:21, that "the LORD God made garments of skin for Adam and his wife, and clothed them." Genesis 4:4 indicates that Abel was offering animal sacrifices as a means of worship. Genesis 6:7 indicates that animals would perish in the flood. The first reference to using animals for food is after the flood, when God said to Noah's family, "Every moving thing that is alive shall be food for you; I give all to you, as I gave the green plant" (Genesis 9:3). Whether this implies that the human race were vegetarians up until this time is a matter of debate; but even if so, this does not necessarily mean that animal death is the result of the curse in Genesis 3. Actually one looks in vain for any specific basis in Scripture for such a view. There is no reason to think human sin had anything to do with animal death, or that animal death is abnormal and is part of the curse upon sin.

My conclusion is that death is natural for plants and animals. I take it to be part of the creation's *benefit* for human beings. It is part of what is meant by "subduing the earth" (Genesis 1:28). Such death is the source of food, wood, fuel, clothes, oil, and other such benefits.

Human death, however, is another story—a completely DIFFERENT story! From the very beginning it has been clear that human death is *unnatural*; it is a CURSE upon sin. See this warning in Genesis 2:17: "But from the tree of the knowledge of good and evil you shall not eat, for in the day that you eat from it you will surely die." See also Ezekiel 18:4, 20, "The person who sins will die" (God's Word translation). "The wages of sin is death" (Romans 6:23).

The man Adam was the first human being, and in that role he acted as the representative for the entire human race. Thus when Adam our representative sinned, he brought the curse of death on the entire human race. Romans 5 says this in several ways: "Through one man sin entered into the world, and death through sin" (v. 12). "By the transgression of the one the many died" (v. 15). "By the transgression of the one, death reigned through the one" (v. 17). First Corinthians 15:22 sums it up: "In Adam all die." This was first announced in Genesis 3:19, where God pronounced the curse of death upon sin as soon as it began – "For you are dust, and to dust you shall return." This placed the entire human race under "slavery to corruption" (Romans 8:21).

Despite the fact that we all die, this was never supposed to happen! Human death was not a part of God's plan and purpose for us. We were supposed to live forever! How often have you heard, "He/she died of 'natural causes.'" NO! There is nothing natural about human death! Even *old age* is not natural for us human beings!

II. THE THREE FORMS OF HUMAN DEATH

Human death has three forms, i.e., sinners die in three different ways as the result of their sin and of the Adamic curse. I will explain each one of them here.

A. Spiritual death of the soul.

The first kind of death applies to the soul or spirit (which are two different words for our spiritual part). This was the first kind of death to be experienced by a human being. Remember that God warned Adam in the Garden of Eden not to eat of the tree of knowledge of good and evil. Here are His words (Genesis 2:17): "For in the **day** that you eat from it you will surely **die**." This does not refer to the death of Adam's body, for that did not happen until 930 years later (Genesis 5:5). But we know from New Testament teaching that *all* sinners are dead in a spiritual sense while their bodies are still alive, and this is most likely that to which God is referring in Genesis 2:17.

Several New Testament texts speak of this spiritual death. Paul says in Ephesians 2:1, 5 that when we were sinners, we were "dead in [our] trespasses and sins …. We were dead in our transgressions." In Colossians 2:13 he repeats that sinners are "dead in [their] trespasses." In Luke 15:24 the prodigal son's father describes his son's lost state as a state of spiritual death: "For this son of mine was dead and has come to life again; he was lost and has been found." In 1 Timothy 5:6 Paul says the worldly widow "is dead even while she lives."

Though a sinner's soul is in a state of death, it still exists and functions. This shows that we should not think that death always results in destruction and non-existence. Some assume that when someone or something is said to be dead, it becomes totally inert and immediately begins to decay and ultimately will dissolve and disappear. That is because they assume that the way the BODY dies is the way everything dies. But that is not so. The concept of death has other connotations. For example, when a vehicle's battery loses it charge, we say it is DEAD. But that does not mean it begins to rot and dissolve. Thus it is with the soul of the sinner. It still exists as an entity, but is dead.

What, then, is the essence of death? We can describe it as *separation* from the source of LIFE. We will remember from our first lesson, "The Living God," that God alone is the source of all life. But sin separates the sinner from life-giving contact with God. Thus the unbelieving sinner's soul is dead because his or her connection with the source of life – God – is broken. Ephesians 2:12 describes sinners as being "separate from Christ … having no hope and without God in the world." Then in Ephesians

4:18 he makes it even more clear when he says that sinners are "excluded from the life of God." To be without God is to be without spiritual life.

B. Physical death of the *body*.

Now we turn to the second kind of human death, the physical death of the body. In human beings, the life of the body is connected with the presence of the soul within the body. This means that the physical death of the body occurs when the spirit leaves the body. James 2:26 says that "the body apart from the spirit is dead."

The death of this body *does* result in its decay and non-existence. This process begins at the moment the death occurs. The same does not happen to the spirit, though. When death overtakes our bodies, our souls continue to be alive and conscious, perpetuating our identity as the person we are. When our body dies, our soul/spirit does not die. It *experiences* the body's death, to be sure, and it is affected by the death of the body. What is the main way the soul is affected by the body's death? From that moment on, until the second coming of Jesus, the soul exists *without a body* in the invisible angelic universe where God appears before His angels on a throne. You will be existing there as a bodiless spirit. So what's wrong with this? That's the way *angels* exist all the time, isn't it? Yes, but that's *natural* for angels. It is NOT natural for us! Our spirits were never intended to exist apart from a body! So —

This is one reason why this physical death—the body's decay and the soul's bodiless existence—is unnatural; it is part of the curse upon sin. Without a body, the person is incomplete. In 2 Corinthians 5:1-10, Paul compares it with a person in this life being naked or unclothed; he compares it with not having a dwelling to live in. Our soul does not suffer because of this, but we will still sense that something is missing in our lives—and we will continue to do so until we (as a naked soul) are clothed with a new glorified body at the second coming of Jesus.

If we are saved when we die physically, we will indeed receive that glorified body, unlike those who die when they are lost. That means that we who are saved will have suffered only two forms of death during our existence: the spiritual death of our pre-Christian state, and the physical death of our body. But there is still a third kind of death, one which only the lost will suffer.

C.   Eternal death of the *person*.

The third kind of death is the *eternal* death of the lost in hell, which will affect the entire person, body and spirit. At the second coming even lost sinners will receive a reconstituted body, the nature of which is not revealed in Scripture. However, it will not be a glorified body fit for living in our final heaven forever. According to Daniel 12:2, those who receive the unglorified bodies will be resurrected "to disgrace and everlasting contempt."

The eternal death experienced by the lost is called the "second death" in Revelation 20:14-15 and Revelation 21:8. More specifically, it is called the second death in *the lake of fire*. It is called *eternal* death because it is the state in which the lost will exist **forever**. This is hell. It never ends. Some Bible scholars teach the false doctrine that the sinner's death in hell cannot be eternal just because it is a place of *death*, and (so they say) we all know that dead things rot away and disappear. Thus those cast into hell will either immediately or ultimately be annihilated and burned up and thus will cease to exist. But this is simply not true. We saw earlier, in discussing spiritual death, that death is not always a state of ceasing to exist. This applies to this eternal death as well as to that spiritual death.

The lost person's eternal existence is called a state of DEATH for two reasons. First of all, it is called death simply because it is the result of SIN. Death is what we get when we sin (Romans 6:23). It is a state of punishment for sin. Second, it is called death because the essence of the second death is eternal *separation from God*, the source of life – and such separation is exactly what death is. In Matthew 7:23, Jesus says to the lost, **"Depart from me,** you who practice lawlessness." We learn in Matthew 25:41 that on the Judgment Day God will say to the lost, **"Depart from me,** accursed ones, into the eternal fire which has been prepared for the devil and his angels." Then in 2 Thessalonians 1:9 we hear these terrifying words, that the lost will "pay the penalty of eternal destruction, **away from the presence of the Lord** and from the glory of His power."

I want to emphasize this again: this eternal "death" does not involve destruction in the sense of non-existence. The word used for "destruction" in 2 Thessalonians 1:9 (*olethros*) also has the meanings of ruin, corruption, and loss. It is the state of eternal separation from God, the source of life, and thus the loss of everything that is meant by and derived from the possession of life.

III. HUMAN DEATH IS OUR ENEMY.

In Acts 17 we read about Paul and his fellow-missionary, Silas, doing their missionary preaching in Thessalonica. Verse 3 says that they were preaching the *death and resurrection* of Christ. Many pagans were converted, but many were not. The latter group were extremely upset by what Paul and Silas were doing. These unbelievers formed a mob and sought to get this little pocket of Christians arrested. They accused Paul and Silas of "turning the world upside down" by preaching the death and resurrection of Christ.

Ironically, these rabble-rousers were right about one thing: Paul and Silas *were* causing a revolution! They *were* bringing about a *complete reversal* of the present world order. But the mob was wrong in this respect: the world is *already UPSIDE DOWN!* Paul and Silas were simply turning it *RIGHTSIDE UP* again!

You see, we do in fact live in a world where not life, but DEATH reigns like a king. We live in a dying world, a world permeated by death! It's like living and walking "in the valley of the shadow of death," as the 23rd Psalm says. Death is so common and universal that we are numbed into thinking it is normal and natural; we have just accepted the upside-down notion that "this is the way it has always been, and this is the way it's supposed to be." I.e., we are like the Thessalonians to which Paul and Silas were preaching: we don't get it – that the world where death reigns is already *upside down*.

This is how Paul puts it in Romans 5:14, 17. Because of the sin of the first man Adam, death has *reigned as king* since that time. In the Garden of Eden, death usurped power and control over the human race, and it became an evil tyrant over our lives. Since that time our universe has been "subjected to futility" and meaninglessness; it is in a state of "bondage to decay" (Romans 8:18-21). It is groaning and straining for things to be set right again.

In the final lesson in this series we will explain the "setting right." For now we will just look a bit more into this subject of the upside-down condition of our world, emphasizing that *death is our enemy*.

In what ways is this so? Here we will be using Hebrews 2:14-15, which says: "Therefore, since the children share in flesh and blood, He Himself likewise also partook of the same, that through death He might render powerless him who had the power of death, that is, the devil, and might free those who through fear of death were subject to slavery all their lives." Here we see that death is our enemy for the following reasons.

A.   In this life, we live in constant *fear of death*.

Verse 15 above refers to this "fear of death." See also Psalms 55:4 – "My heart is in anguish within me, and the terrors of death have fallen upon me." This fear of death may have many causes: fear of nothingness, fear of the unknown, fear of pain, fear of separation from loved ones.

But mostly, consciously or not, this fear is the result of knowing there is a Judgment Day ahead. As Hebrews 9:27 says, "It is appointed for men to die once and after this comes judgment." As 1 Corinthians 15:56 says, "The sting of death is sin." In the last verses of Romans 1, the Apostle Paul gives a long list of the sins that sinners love to commit. Then in verse 32 he says that "they know the ordinance of God, that those who practice such things are worthy of death." And in this text he is speaking specifically of pagans who never saw a Bible, but still have the "work of the law written in their hearts" (Romans 2:15). In their heart of hearts they can sense that they are sinners who will have to face God in judgment someday.

Psychologists and psychiatrists assert that fear of death is universal; some say it is "the instinctual root of all other fears." Anthropologist Ernest Becker argues that "the idea of death, the fear of it, haunts the human animal like nothing else; it is the mainspring of human activity — activity designed largely to avoid the fatality of death, to overcome it by denying in some way that it is the final destiny for man." (From an online article, "The Universal Fear of Death That Haunts Living Minds." See www.atmostfear-enterainment.com.) The famous secular humanist Corliss Lamont said, in his later years, "Today, more than ever, I feel the haunting sense of transiency. If only time would for a while come to a stop…. I sympathize with everyone who has ever longed for immortality and I wish that the enchanting dream of eternal life could indeed come true."

B.   Because of the fear of death, we live in *slavery* to death.

Hebrews 2:15 refers to "those who through fear of death were **subject to slavery** all their lives." Or as the ESV says, "subject to lifelong slavery." After all, what is life all about? People have many diverse notions about this. But in the final analysis (literally), it pretty much comes down to the same thing for everyone: The dominant purpose of life on this earth seems to be: trying to avoid death.

We are slaves of death because its forerunners or predecessors or precursors spread like tentacles through all our days, long before we reach that final event itself. We are in constant battle with the forerunners of death. What are they? Diseases such as cancer, arthritis, polio, leukemia, heart disease, diabetes, Alzheimer's, Parkinson's, measles, glaucoma, AIDS, emphysema, scoliosis, malaria. These things are just getting us warmed up for death—priming the pump for death. We can mention also things like birth defects, accidents, broken bones, starvation, pain as such in any form. What are the only certainties in life? DEATH and taxes. We are reminded of this every time we pass a cemetery or attend a funeral.

We are slaves of death because a major part of life's time and money are spent on health care, safety, and insurance. How much of your budget is actually spent on such things as medicine, doctor's appointments, hospital stays, exercise equipment, insurance bills, taxes to fund social programs like Obamacare and Medicaid? In 2014 nearly 30% of the federal budget was for health care. Think how much money is spent on research to deal with all these things!

Here's another consideration: we are slaves of death because death places an absolute limit on life, leading to a sense of meaninglessness. Death is a sure thing, no matter how hard you fight against it. Not many can plan more than a few decades ahead, and *no one* can plan 100 years or 1000 years ahead. Such thoughts generate feelings of pessimism and meaninglessness and a "Who cares?" attitude. Someone drew a cartoon of a sign that says "DEAD END." Someone had put graffiti on it: "WHAT ISN'T?"

Whether we realize it or not, we are *dominated by death*. We are in mortal combat with our enemy, death. As a medieval saying puts it: "In the midst of life we are surrounded by death."

C. Death is our enemy because it is a *tool of Satan.*

See Hebrews 2:14 again. The devil is described as the one who has "the power of death." How is this so? The weirdness of death and the fear of death make it inevitable that we human beings will look desperately for ways to come to terms with death, or reconcile our minds to it. We will look for ways to become *friends* with death. This makes us vulnerable to Satan's deceits, and deception is the main way Satan attacks us.

This inherent enmity between us and death makes it an ideal weapon for Satan to use against us, an ideal tool in Satan's toolkit. He uses our fear of death as an entry point into our lives. He uses it to lead us away from God and down the roads of sin and falsehood. This universal fear of death gives him the *perfect opportunity* to concoct a whole encyclopedia of *lies* and *phony solutions* to the death problem. To help us suppress our fear of death, Satan leads us into all sorts of lies and deception, trying to give us false hope concerning death. He does this to try to lead us away from the only true solution to this problem. He is like a slick salesman who persuades us to buy counterfeit goods.

Here are some examples of the phony solutions to death with which Satan has deceived millions:

- Evolutionism. This false worldview gives us reason to believe that death is natural, that it is just a part of life. After all, in a chance universe, "whatever is, is good." BUT THIS IS A LIE!

- Occultism, in many of its forms. E.g., spiritism, whose basic theme is *There Is No Death*. This is the title of a book I had in my library explaining spiritism. Another book was titled, *Death: The Gateway to Life*. Another occult theme is reincarnation. In the western world, including the New Age Movement, reincarnation is sold as a way of not worrying about death. You will come back again. One more occult example is the celebration of Halloween. This was originally *and still is* a witchcraft holiday. It is based on the Festival of Samhain, "the lord of the dead." It is built around death symbols: skeletons, ghosts, coffins, tombstones, skull & crossbones, mummies, and graveyards.

- Near-death experiences, or life-after-life experiences. I believe that many of these are either caused by or exploited by Satan and his demons to give false hope of the afterlife.

- Hedonism ("eat, drink, and be merry, for tomorrow you die"). This is often the opposite of reincarnation. I.e., "You only live once; make the best of it!"

These are examples of what Isaiah 28:15 calls "covenants with death" – agreements with death – "Because you have said, 'We have made a covenant with death, and with Sheol we have an agreement, when the overwhelming whip passes through it will not come to us, for we have made lies our refuge; and in falsehood we have taken shelter'" (ESV). But will they work? NO! These are just Satan's lies! The only solution to the problem of death is JESUS! If you are counting on anything but Jesus to rescue you from death, listen to Isaiah 28:18: "Then your covenant with death will be annulled and your agreement with Sheol will not stand; when the overwhelming scourge passes through, you will be beaten down by it" (ESV).

But if you are standing on the Rock that is Jesus Christ, you are protected from this deadly enemy. How is this so? This leads us to the final lesson in this series.

A MATTER OF LIFE AND DEATH

PART FOUR: THE DEATH OF DEATH

INTRODUCTION

Our theme in this series of lessons is "A Matter of Life and Death." We started with an explanation of the source of all life: the Living God. Then came a look at the forms of life God created: angelic, physical, and human. But then, we saw how sin brought DEATH to the human race, turning our lives upside down. Now what? Do you think that God, the Creator of Life, is going to let this phony tyrant—King Death—just take over his creation without a fight? NO!

What we are doing in this lesson is showing how God's plan of salvation is to confront and defeat this enemy, DEATH, in a battle to the death! His plan is to put death to death! The result of God's counter-attack is none other than: *THE DEATH OF DEATH!*

PART ONE. THE DEATH AND RESURRECTION OF JESUS

The death of death is something that can be accomplished only through Jesus Christ, the true King of life and death. Here we will see exactly how He has done that.

I. JESUS SOLVED THE PROBLEM OF DEATH.

When I think of the Logos, God the Son, coming into the world that first time, I think of the beloved cartoon character of my youth, MIGHTY MOUSE. His theme song:

> *"Mr. Trouble never hangs around, when he hears this mighty sound: 'HERE I COME TO SAVE THE DAY!' That means that Mighty Mouse is on the way!"*

This can be Jesus' theme song: **HERE I COME TO SAVE THE DAY!** I have not watched Mighty Mouse for a very long time, but I do have a new T-shirt that has a similar message. It shows Jesus and a group of superheroes sitting on a high-up construction eyebar (or something similar). Jesus is sitting in the middle, surrounded by Batman, Captain America, The Hulk, The Flash (holding a big Bible), Superman, and a guy with yellow skin that I cannot identify, plus Spiderman hanging upside down. While His audience is reverently concentrating, Jesus is shown speaking these words: "… and that's how I saved the world." I love to wear that shirt when I leave my cave!

That is indeed the very purpose for which Jesus came into the world: To *save the day*—actually, to save the WORLD—by confronting and defeating DEATH, and by restoring LIFE to its rightful dominance in the creation. See 2 Timothy 1:10. This verse says specifically that God's purpose has "been revealed by the appearing of our Savior Christ Jesus, who **abolished death** and brought life and immortality to light through the gospel." How did He do it?

First, to defeat death He had to conquer the devil himself. First John 3:8 says that "The Son of God appeared for this purpose, to destroy the works of the devil." And remember Hebrews 2:14-15: "Therefore, since the children share in flesh and blood, He Himself likewise also partook of the same, that through death He might render powerless him who had the power of death, that is, the devil, and might free those who through fear of death were subject to slavery all their lives."

But dealing with the devil was not the only thing involved in Christ's purpose. In the most general sense, His mission was all about **banishing death** and **restoring life**. See these texts:

- John 10:10 – "I came that they may have life, and have it abundantly."
- Acts 3:15 – He came as "the Prince of Life," or "the author of life."
- John 6:33, 35, 41 – "For the bread of God is that which comes down out of heaven, and gives life to the world…. I am the bread of life…. I am the bread that came down out of heaven."
- John 1:4 – "In Him was life, and the life was the Light of men."
- John 14:6 – "I am the … life."
- John 11:25 – "I am the resurrection and the life."
- Colossians 3:4 – Paul refers to "Christ, who is our life."

I don't really think of Jesus as Mighty Mouse. In view of these texts, I would much rather think of Him as MIGHTY LIFE! He came to "save the day" by *putting death to death*, by taking away *death* and giving us *life*. And how did He do this?

II. JESUS SUFFERED THE PAINS OF DEATH.

The first way Jesus solved the problem of death is that He suffered the *pains* of death. See Acts 2:24, which is talking about Jesus. In the NKJV it reads that Jesus is the one "whom God raised up, having loosed the **pains** of death, because it was not possible that He should be held by it." (Other versions say "the pangs of death" [ESV], and "the agony of death [NASB, NIV]. The Greek is *ōdin*, "birth pains.")

In this verse Peter says that God raised Jesus from the dead, "having loosed" Him from the pains of death. It is interesting that "having loosed" is an aorist participle, which usually means that the action of the participle takes place *prior to* the action of the main verb, which here is "raised up." This suggests that even while in the tomb, Jesus had already been loosed from the pains of death in some sense. This makes me think that the word "death" here is being used in a comprehensive sense, general enough to refer to everything Jesus was going through on the cross, that resulted in His death. On the cross, just before He bowed His head and died, He uttered, "It is finished" (John 19:30). His suffering had ended. The pains of death are just about over. Jesus had taken on the enemy *death* in all its forms, and had overcome it. His coming forth from the tomb alive is His victory march.

From another perspective we can think of Jesus's mission as involving a kind of "prize fight" with the devil—winner take all. In this battle there was a lot of preliminary sparring and jabbing (during Jesus's earthly ministry), until Jesus landed the winning combination of punches. The cross was Jesus's first blow in his knock-out, one-two combo against Satan. Jesus landed this first punch by dying on the cross! As strange as this might sound, Jesus had to *die* to win this fight against death and Satan. Remember Hebrews 2:14, which says that Jesus became a human being so that "**through death** He might render powerless him who had the power of death, that is, the devil." And so, as Isaiah 53:12 prophesied, "He poured out his life unto death" (NIV).

In order to save us, Jesus had to suffer the very deaths that threaten us. And He did it in our place, for us, as our substitute or stand-in. Hebrews 2:9 says that "He tasted death for every human being." Notice that in the beginning of this paragraph I put it into plural form, "deaths." This is because, in His saving work, Jesus defeated all forms of death. He died *physically* in His human nature, and He suffered the agonies of *eternal* death (hell itself) in his divine nature. He took it all upon Himself, as our substitute – all in our place!

What this means for us is simply this. As Christians who have accepted Jesus as our Lord and Savior, we are resting in His grace now and forever. Our sins are covered by the suffering He endured to pay the penalty we deserve for them. We are justified by His blood (Romans 5:9). Therefore we have been freed from the threat of the eternal second death in the lake of fire! There is therefore now no condemnation for us, because we are *in Christ Jesus*, who has already suffered that second death in our place. Hallelujah!

III. JESUS BROKE OPEN THE PRISON OF DEATH, BY HIS RESURRECTION.

At first, with Jesus on the cross and then in the tomb, it seemed as if Satan had won – as if Satan had locked Jesus up in the prison of death, in a prison cell. On that crucifixion Friday and post-crucifixion Saturday I can see Satan staring at Jesus behind the bars of death, saying, "GOTCHA!"

But remember, in this battle against Satan, in this prize fight, the *death* of Jesus is just the first punch of a winning combination. Jesus has not thrown the second part of the one-two combo yet. But that does happen on the third day, Sunday, when Jesus rises from the dead! In this fight, the resurrection was Jesus's "haymaker," His "Sunday punch," if you please! It was the **death blow** to Satan, and the **death blow** to death itself.

Remember Acts 2:24, which says that Jesus is the one "whom God raised up, having loosed the **pains** of death, because it was not possible that He should be **held** by it." Remember the Easter hymn: "Death could not keep its prey – He tore the bars away!" Here I always think of an old Tarzan movie where he bent the prison bars in order to escape the bad guys that had captured him. Just as Tarzan was "stronger than steel," Jesus was *stronger than death!*

See Revelation 1:17-18 also, where the risen Christ says to the Apostle John, "Do not be afraid; I am the first and the last, and the living One; and I was dead, and behold, I am alive forevermore, and I have the keys of death and of Hades." (The word "Hades" stands for the realm of death.) Here I picture Jesus, "trapped" in the prison cell of death, watching through the bars as Satan dances a jig of joy outside while mockingly dangling the keys of death in Jesus's face. Then suddenly Jesus grabs a couple of the prison bars, and easily bends them apart. Then He delivers His knockout punch to the devil, snatches up the keys and hold them aloft, and shouts for all the world to hear: "I was dead, and behold, I am alive forevermore, and I have the keys of death and of Hades"! That He has the *keys* to death and the place of death means that now HE has the power over death—because of His resurrection!

Now, Jesus can use these keys to set everyone else free from death's prison. See Matthew 12:29. Here Jesus is explaining how He has the power to set people free from demon possession. He says: "Or how can anyone enter the strong man's house and carry off his property, unless he first binds the strong man? And then he will plunder his house." We can broaden this from just exorcisms to represent the entire battle of Christ against Satan:

- The strong man is Satan.
- The strong man's house is the prison of death.
- The strong man's property is all the lost sinners, who are in bondage to death.
- The Rescuer is Jesus. (In Luke 4:18 Jesus says He was sent into this world "to proclaim release to the captives, and … to set free those who are oppressed.")
- Entering the house stands for Jesus's crucifixion.
- Binding the strong man stands for Jesus's resurrection. (Here Jesus takes the strong man's keys, and unlocks the prison of death from the inside!)
- Carrying off the strong man's property is the salvation of sinners from death!

PART TWO. THE DEATH OF DEATH
FOR THE CHRISTIAN

Now we want to look at the death of death in the Christian's life. Here's the point: everything Jesus did, He did for us. He died for us, He arose for us, He defeated death and Satan for us. If you want to be saved from all the forms of death – spiritual, physical, eternal – you MUST be joined with Christ in true faith and repentance, you must confess your faith in Him, and you must meet Him in Christian baptism. When you do this, you begin to share in the spoils of Christ's victory! Which are —

I.   THE PENALTY OF DEATH IS REMOVED.

The first aspect of death that is put to death in our Christian experience is the *penalty* for our sin, i.e., eternal death in the lake of fire. When we meet Jesus in Christian baptism, we experience there the death of this death: our ETERNAL death (hell) is gone! This is because in baptism, our sin-debt of eternity in hell is forgiven. We are justified. Jesus paid the penalty of eternal condemnation in hell for us. No eternal death for you!

God can cancel this death-debt for us because Jesus broke the connection between sin and death, as Romans 8:1-4 teaches. The first two verses here say this: "Therefore there is now no condemnation for those who are in Christ Jesus. For the law of the Spirit of life in Christ Jesus has set you free from the law of sin and of death." Here, the *law* of "sin and death" is the declaration of God that *sin is always followed by death*, as Romans 6:23 says. But "the law of the Spirit of life" has *replaced* that law for Christians! We are sinners, but the threat and fear of eternal death no longer hangs over us! There is *no condemnation* for those who are in Christ Jesus!

II.   THE POWER OF DEATH IS REMOVED.

The second aspect of death that dies when we become Christians is the *power* of death. This is because, again in baptism, we receive the Holy Spirit of Life (Romans 8:2) to take away our *spiritual* death. This is still a work of Jesus Christ, since it was Jesus on the day of Pentecost who poured forth the Holy Spirit upon the church, according to Acts 2:33: "Therefore having been exalted to the right hand of God, and having received from the Father the promise of the Holy Spirit, He has poured forth this which you both see and hear." Now that the Holy Spirit has come, He was and is ready to enter into the body and soul of any sinner who obeys the gospel.

Before we were Christians, we were in the state of spiritual death, i.e., our souls were "dead in our trespasses and sins," and we were unable to please God by obeying his laws of holiness for our lives. We were in a state of spiritual weakness because, as Romans 8:7-8 says, "the mind set on the flesh is hostile toward God; for it does not subject itself to the law of God, for it is not even able to do so, and those who are in the flesh cannot please God." But by the presence and power of the Holy Spirit given in baptism, that old flesh-oriented "mind," that "old self," dies (Romans 6:6), and now we have the power to obey God's laws and commandments. (See Romans 8:5-13.)

Paul explains this in Romans 6:1-5, where he shows us that in baptism our old life dies and is buried, and we rise to new LIFE. Here is what he says:

> What shall we say then? Are we to continue in sin so that grace may increase? May it never be! How shall we who died to sin still live in it? Or do you not know that all of us who have been baptized into Christ Jesus have been baptized into His death? Therefore we have been buried with Him through baptism into death, so that as Christ was raised from the dead through the glory of the Father, so we too might walk in newness of life. For if we have become united with Him in the likeness of His death, certainly we shall also be in the likeness of His resurrection.

Here is what is happening in baptism. When you enter the water, your spirit (which is your soul) is in a state of spiritual death because of your sinfulness. But in that moment you are in the water, the Holy Spirit takes on the role of *mortician*: He receives your dead soul for burial, and BURIES it in Christian baptism, where its deadness remains buried. In a sense you can say that your "dead soul" is left behind in baptism.

Therefore you come up out of the baptismal water with a NEW (*renewed*) soul or spirit— a spiritual nature that is ALIVE. Romans 8:10 says "the spirit is alive because of righteousness" (God's righteousness). Now you are ready and able to "walk in newness of life"! You have literally "passed out of death into life"!! (John 5:24)

It is as if you went into the water "unplugged" into the divine socket of life; and in baptism the Holy Spirit plugs you into that life socket again! Now the power of life is flowing into us—and this is *the power of Jesus' resurrection!* In Philippians 3:10 Paul says one of his greatest desires is "that I may know Him and the power of His resurrection"!

So to sum up, here is what happens when you surrender your life to Christ: the power of death is removed, and the power of life now flows through you. This power of life is the power of the Holy Spirit who is dwelling in you. He is called the "Spirit of life" (Romans 8:2). He is called the "water of life" (John 4:14; 7:38). Jesus says in John 6:63, "The Spirit gives life." He has given it to you. So what? The effect is that we now have a different kind of power: the power to obey God's commandments for holy living.

III. THE PRESENCE OF DEATH IS REMOVED.

We next experience the Death of Death when the very *presence* of death is removed—or maybe more precisely, when WE are removed from the presence of death. Ironically, this happens at the moment of physical death. This is ironic because all our lives we are living in the presence of death. This includes physical death in all its forms: we suffer the "little deaths" of such things as defects and disease; we suffer through the death of loved ones; we live in dread of our own death. It includes spiritual death also. We see sin and its horrible results in the lives of others; we ourselves struggle against that spiritual death that we buried behind in Christian baptism. I.e., like the "walking dead," that old corpse seems to be sticking its dead hand up out if its grave to the surface and grabbing and pulling at our ankles, trying to pull us back into a life of sin again.

As long as we are in this world, we are surrounded by death. We feel like crying out with Paul (Romans 7:24) – "O wretched man that I am! Who will set me free from the body of this death?" We have the *foretaste* of that deliverance from the time of our baptism, but death is still all around us – *until that moment of physical death*!

In the moment of physical death our spirits are separated from our bodies, *and* are separated from this death-cursed world itself. That's the moment when we (our spirits) will be transported into our temporary heavenly home. What are the blessings we will experience there? There we will be in the angelic heaven, in the presence of a manifestation of God the Father; in the presence of the glorified, resurrected Jesus; in the presence of the souls of the other believers who have died; and yes: with angels all around! How different this will be from this world of death! And this will be our home, where we will dwell as "unclothed spirits," until the second coming of Jesus.

But the most important thing of all about this transition at physical death is this: At this moment all vestiges of sin and spiritual death are cleansed from our spirits. See Hebrews 12:23, which refers to "the spirits of the righteous made perfect." That's what we all want to be the case now, but: "The spirit is willing, but the flesh is weak." But one day this weak flesh will be left behind, and God will make our spirits perfect. That will be the day of our physical death. On that day, we will be rescued from the presence of death as such; we will be gone from the worldly environment of sin and death; we will be in the presence of glory.

But here's the deal. As wonderful as it is thus far—with the penalty of death, the power of death, and the presence of death DEAD AND GONE—still, this is not the final stage of the death of death. There is one more step, and that is what comes next.

IV. THE PERIL OF DEATH IS REMOVED.

The last step in the death of death is that the *peril* of death is now gone forever. Following the second coming, our bodily resurrection, and the Judgment Day, we will be moved to our final and eternal dwelling place, the New Heavens and New Earth. Revelation 21:4 gives us this promise, that in that day God "will wipe away every tear from their eyes; and there will no longer be any death; there will no longer be any mourning, or crying, or pain; the first things have passed away."

At the resurrection from the dead, we will receive new, glorified bodies, and the last enemy—death—will be abolished. See 1 Corinthians 15:25-26, 54. Verse 25 says Jesus "must reign until He has put all His enemies under His feet." Then verse 26 zeroes in on one of these enemies: "The last enemy that will be abolished is death." As verse 54 says, "But when this perishable will have put on the imperishable, and this mortal will have put on immortality, then will come about the saying that is written, "DEATH IS SWALLOWED UP in victory." That is the day when "what is mortal will be swallowed up by life" (2 Corinthians 5:4). When we get our new bodies, we will no longer be "naked souls," but will be full persons again, this time for eternity. Our perfected souls will be clothed with glorified bodies just like the one Jesus now has (Philippians 3:21; 1 John 3:2).

In that final heaven, i.e., the New Heavens and New Earth, we will dwell in the presence of a manifestation of the Living God, and in the presence of Jesus the Lamb of God, who made it all possible. Revelation 21:3 says, "And I heard a loud voice from the throne, saying, 'Behold, the tabernacle of God is among men, and He will dwell among them, and they shall be His people, and God Himself will be among them." Revelation 22:1-4 adds,

> Then he showed me a river of the water of life, clear as crystal, coming from the throne of God and of the Lamb, in the middle of its street. On either side of the river was the **tree of life,** bearing twelve kinds *of* fruit, yielding its fruit every month; and the leaves of the tree were for the healing of the nations. There will no longer be any curse; and **the throne of God and of the Lamb will be in it,** and His bond-

servants will serve Him; they will see His face, and His name will be on their foreheads."

But there is one final thing to point out about the New Heavens and New Earth: *there will be no threat of DEATH for us, ever again!* This is indeed one great blessing of the New Earth: the danger and peril of death are gone. Revelation 21:4 specifically says, "And He will wipe away every tear from their eyes, and there will no longer be any death." Revelation 22:3 says, "There will no longer be any curse," at the center of which is human death. The peril of death in all its forms and with all of its consequences is *gone!* There will be no hunger or thirst (Revelation 7:16) and no tears (Revelation 7:17; 21:4). See again the entire content of verse 21:4 – "And He will wipe away every tear from their eyes; and there will no longer be any death; there will no longer be any mourning, or crying, or pain; the first things have passed away." Instead of these things, we will have access to –

- The Tree of Life – Revelation 2:7; 22:2.
- The "river of the water of life" – Revelation 22:1ff.; also 7:17; 21:6; 22:17.
- The visible presence of the Living God Himself! – Revelation 21:4; 22:1-5
- The Living Christ—who made it all possible – Revelation 21:22-23, 22:3-4.

CONCLUSION

The death of death! Don't you want to live forever in a world where death is dead? That's what God offers you. As Christians, you already have this hope, if you remain faithful. See James 1:12 – "Blessed is a man who perseveres under trial; for once he has been approved, he will receive the **crown of life** which *the Lord* has promised to those who love Him." Heed Revelation 2:10 – "Be faithful until death, and I will give you a crown of **life.**"

This is the choice God gives you: Deuteronomy 30:19, "I call heaven and earth to witness against you today, that I have set before you life and death, the blessing and the curse. So choose life in order that you may live." And Jeremiah 21:8, "Thus says the LORD, 'Behold, I set before you the way of life and the way of death.'" **Choose life!**

SECTION TWO

THE NATURE
OF MAN

MAN IS 100% CREATED

After answering a question on the origin of the human soul, I was motivated to share some thoughts on the fact that human beings are created beings in every aspect of their nature. This material is taken mostly from my book, *The Faith Once for All*, chapter 6, "The Nature of Man."

It is very important to understand that a human being is wholly a creature; both body and spirit have been created by God. The doctrine of *ex nihilo* creation as such is unique to the Bible; therefore the doctrine of man as a created being is unique to Scripture also. In every non-biblical world view at least a part of man is eternal, and in some it is divine. In materialistic monism all matter is eternal; man is simply one stage in the eternal chance evolution of eternal stuff. In spiritualistic monism (e.g., Hinduism) the body is usually not even regarded as real, and the spirit is a part of or is identical with the eternal divine spirit. Pagan dualism usually regards matter—and thus the body—as real but as evil and temporary, but it regards the spirit as eternal and often divine. Over against all such false doctrines the Bible affirms the full creaturehood of man. Only God is eternal, immortal, and uncreated (John 1:3; Romans 1:25; 1 Timothy 1:17; 6:16). (See the addendum for some examples of pagan dualism.)

Despite this clear biblical affirmation, it is not uncommon for sincere Christians to naively assume that the soul or spirit is a divine spark or a little piece of God, and somehow inherently eternal and immortal and even divine. Alexander Campbell has said, "Lord, what is man? Thine own offspring, reared out of the dust of earth, inspired with a portion of thine own spirit." Thus man has "something in common with God"; there is "a divinity stirring within him" ("An Address on Colleges," *Millennial Harbinger*, February 1854; College Press reprint, 25:63-64). C. C. Crawford (*Survey Course in Christian Doctrine*, College Press, I:142-143) has said that man's body "was a divine creation; whereas the spirit that was breathed into it was a divine gift." What does this mean? Crawford explains that in Genesis 2:7 God implants a spirit in the body by "stooping down and placing His lips and nostrils to the inanimate form which he had created, and then expelling an infinitesimal portion of His very own essence into it." Stanley Sayers ("Life After Death," *Gospel Light*, September 1983, p. 132) says that in light of Genesis 2:7 the soul must survive death because "you cannot destroy the God-part!"

Others within the broad scope of Christendom say that man was not *created* divine but will somehow *become* divine as the climax of the salvation process. This idea is at the heart of Mormon soteriology, and it appears occasionally in more orthodox circles. Texts such as Philippians 3:21 and 1 John 3:2, which say that in the resurrection we will be like Christ, are misapplied to his divine nature instead of to his glorified *human* nature. Another text says that we become "partakers of the divine nature" (2 Peter 1:4), but this refers to our ethical oneness with God, not a sharing in the divine essence. I.e., we share his *communicable* attributes such as holiness, love, and patience (see 1 Peter 1:15-16).

The very notion that finite creatures could ever acquire the attributes of infinity is illogical and impossible. Only the transcendent Creator-God is and can be infinite. Creatures should neither desire nor expect to "escape" their finitude, as if this were some kind of unnatural prison. Neither death nor salvation causes us to automatically take on some attribute that belongs exclusively to the infinite Creator. When we die we will not "enter eternity" in the sense that we will no longer be limited by time, nor will we "know fully" (see 1 Corinthians 13:12) by somehow becoming omniscient. We are finite now and will be finite forever.

Divinizing man, either by creation or by salvation, is a most serious false doctrine. It destroys the distinction between God and man, between Creator and creature. It puts man on the same level with God, which is the most basic temptation (Genesis 3:5). It is the height of presumption and arrogance, the epitome of sinful pride. It either debases God or over-exalts man. It destroys the uniqueness of Christ and his incarnation. Nothing of true Christianity remains. See my book, *What the Bible Says About God the Creator*, pp. 151-154.

To say that the spirit or soul is not divine but nevertheless is inherently immortal is not much better. This idea, too, is pagan, not biblical. It denies the full creaturehood of man and the unique eternality of God. Logically it makes man equal with God, since whatever is eternal is indeed divine: God "alone possesses immortality" (1 Timothy 6:16).

The concept of innate immortality has led to false ideas about eternal punishment. Some have said that God created hell not because divine holiness demands it but because the souls of the wicked are indestructible and have to exist *somewhere* for eternity. Others have reacted to this error by teaching an even more serious error. They rightly deny the necessary immortality of the soul, but they then declare that this false idea was what led some in the early church to invent the idea of eternal punishment in the first place, a doctrine which they say is not really taught in the Bible. Thus they deny eternal punishment, believing that their refutation of the "immortal soul" doctrine has removed the basis for it. Examples of this approach are Jehovah's Witnesses and Seventh-day Adventists, who deny not just the immortality of the soul but its very existence; and Restoration Movement writers such as Curtis Dickinson, Russell Boatman, and Edward Fudge.

It is true that because the soul is no less created than the body, the whole being is perishable and destructible. The soul is just as capable of being annihilated and returned to non-existence as the body, but this does not mean that it *must* do so. The fact is that the soul *does not* pass into non-existence at death or at some later point, and this is simply God's will and plan. Though capable of perishing, the soul does not perish at physical death but continues to exist in the temporary absence of a physical body, nor is the sinner's soul annihilated along with a resurrected body after a finite period of punishment in hell. After the resurrection the reunited body and soul will exist forever either in heaven or hell, not of necessity but by God's choice.

Accepting either the divinity or the necessary immortality of the soul leads to a false contrast between soul and body, with an undue elevation of the importance of the soul as compared with the body. It leads to the idea that the soul or spirit is the only valuable part of man, the only real and authentic part, the only part that counts. It is true that the soul or spirit is relatively more important than the body, since it is the aspect of man that is in the image of God. It is also true that this present body is under the curse of sin and death, and must be redeemed (Romans 8:23). But the idea that the body is *by nature* a temporary, unfortunate expedient, while the soul or spirit is *by nature* uncreated and eternal, is quite false.

ADDENDUM

THE NATURE OF MAN IN PAGAN DUALISM (EXAMPLES)

As I indicated above, I am including here a list of some examples of pagan dualism. The term dualism is used in two different ways in this context. It is used for a view called philosophical dualism, and also for a view called anthropological dualism. Philosophical dualism qualifies as a kind of *pagan* dualism because it is the view held by many pagan philosophies and religions, and is absolutely anti-Biblical. It is the idea that all reality is composed of two co-eternal kinds of stuff: physical matter and some kind of spirit, with the latter often being thought of as divine. The Biblical view is totally incompatible with this idea, since it teaches that there is only ONE kind of eternal being, namely, the eternal, immortal God—"He who is the blessed and only Sovereign, the King of kings and Lord of lords, who alone has immortality" (1 Timothy 6:15-16).

Anthropological dualism is a view of the nature of human beings. This view says that all human beings are composed of two distinct kinds of matter or stuff. I.e., their bodies are made of physical matter, and their souls are made of some kind of spiritual stuff. The Biblical view of man falls into this category. The Bible teaches that we are body and spirit. But as the lead essay says above, one hundred person of our dual essence is created. The material stuff of which our bodies are composed is created from nothing, and the spiritual stuff of which our spirits or souls are made is also created from nothing.

Many philosophies and religions hold to the anthropological dualistic view of man, but their views qualify as a *pagan* dualism because they teach that the spiritual part of human beings is eternal and uncreated, and in many cases is thought of as a part of the eternal deity. In the latter case, human beings are part eternal physical matter, and part divine. It should go without saying that this view is anti-biblical.

The shocking truth, however, is that many Christians have adopted a major element of this pagan idea, and hold to what can be called a semi-pagan view of human nature. This is the idea that the human body is made our of created stuff, but the human spirit is actually a little part of the eternal Creator-God of the Bible. This view is often based on a false interpretation of Genesis 2:7. In putting together this list of examples of pagan dualism below, I have included several examples of this semi-paganism from well-known writers and leaders in the Restoration Movement. Let us be on guard against such views as those portrayed here.

I. Pre-Christian Greek mythology: In a common religion called Orphism, one of Zeus's sons—Zagreus (also called Dionysus) as a child was torn to pieces and devoured by an earthly race called Titans. He had run afoul of these Titans and had changed himself into a bull in order to escape them. But they caught the bull, and barbecued it and ate it! Thus particles of Dionysus' divine flesh entered each Titan body. But Zeus then destroyed the whole Titan race, zapping them with a lightning bolt. Their ashes thus contained earthly stuff (the Titans' fried bodies) AND divine stuff (the remains of the body of the god-turned-bull). Out of these ashes the human race was created. Human beings therefore are partly plain old nasty earthly stuff: our physical bodies; and partly a godlike element known as the SOUL.

Because the soul was a particle of the divine, it was, in its own right, immortal, and should never have been mixed with and limited by the body in the first place. But now it is imprisoned in the body and soiled by this contact. Human beings thus long to escape the body and restore the soul to its original state of divine purity.

Orphism thus taught that the body was a prison-house for the soul and a hindrance in the struggle to be free. A phrase in the Greek language was used: *sōma sēma*, "the body is a tomb." This was a common idea in Greek thought. Not only did the body cramp the soul, but, being the Titanic element, it was of evil origin and needed to be suppressed so that the soul could attain freedom. This influenced the rise of asceticism. Earthly life as a whole was rejected. Body and spirit were seen not just as distinct but as hostile to one another. The divine soul is always struggling to be free from the cramping effect of the base, inglorious body. [Taken largely from W. D. Stacey, *The Pauline View of Man* (Macmillan, 1956), pp. 62-63.]

II. The famous Greek philosopher Plato said human beings are "two distinct substances: the thinking soul, which is divine" [or akin to the divine]; and the body. "The soul is a superior substance, inherently indestructible." "It has existed eternally before birth and will exist eternally after death." "The body is composed of the inferior substance called matter," and "is of lower value than the soul." "At death the body simply disintegrates, but the soul returns to 'the heavens.'" "The body is thus the enemy of the soul, for it is a mass of evil, and serves as a prison for the soul." Thus the body is "doomed to total destruction," and there is "no room for the resurrection of the body." [Taken from various sources.]

III. The Greek Stoic philosopher Seneca, a contemporary of Paul, said: "A man is equal to the gods." How? In "his divine soul," which is presently trapped in a physical body. We now bear "the necessary burden of the body," from which our soul longs to be free in death. "When that day comes which shall separate this mixture of human and divine I will leave the body here where I found it and betake myself to the gods." "From the body the soul springs forth ... and never thereafter does it ask what is to befall the husk that it has left behind." It is no more important than clipped hair and fingernails. "It was only your hull." [*The Stoic Philosophy of Seneca*, ed. Moses Hadas (Doubleday Anchor, 1958), 246-7, 252-4.]

IV. Gnosticism: Man "is composed of flesh ... and spirit." Enclosed in the body "is the spirit ... a portion of the divine substance from beyond that has fallen into the world." Alien powers created the human race, trapping the spirit in a fleshly body, just to keep it captive here and prevent it from returning to its real home. "The goal of Gnostic striving is the release of the inner man from the bonds of the world and his return to his native realm of light." ["Gnosticism," *Encyclopedia of Philosophy*, ed. Paul Edwards (Macmillan, 1972 reprint), III:339-40.]

V. Werner Schaafs, a modern Christian writer: "The human spirit is a bit of God's spirit " (from his book, *Theology, Physics, and Miracles* (Canon Press, 1974).]

VI. Restoration Movement [Church of Christ/Christian] writers who have taught this view:

A. Alexander Campbell: "Lord, what is man? Thine own offspring, reared out of the dust of earth, inspired with a portion of thine own spirit." Thus man has "something in common with God." There is "a divinity stirring within him." [*Millennial Harbinger*, February 1854, pp. 63-64]

B. C. C. Crawford: Man's body "was a divine creation; whereas the spirit that was breathed into it was a divine gift." In Genesis 2:7 God implants a spirit in the body when "out of His very own essence He breathed into the hitherto lifeless form all the essential elements of personal life." It pictures "the Creator stooping down and placing His lips and nostrils to the inanimate form which he had created, and then expelling an infinitesimal portion of His very own essence into it." [*Survey Course in Christian Doctrine* (College Press), I:142-43]

C. Don DeWelt: "God breathed into the dead body of Adam a part of Himself or spirit .... All men share the nature of God.... God breathed spirit or a part of Himself into the dead body of the first man." "Since man shares the nature of God man's capacities are limitless!" "The human spirit which is the likeness or image of God comes from God as a part of Himself who is Spirit." [Appendix to Russell Boatman, *What the Bible Says About the End Time* (College Press), pp. 354, 358]

D. Stanley Sayers, printed in *The Banner of Truth*, ed. Fred Blakely, Jan. 1984, p. 4: The Bible teaches "the indestructibility of the immortal soul. God created man from the dust of the ground and 'breathed into his nostrils the breath of life' (Genesis 2:7). Man, made in the very image and likeness of God (Genesis 1:26), is himself immortal [i.e., eternal as to the endlessness of his existence]; not his physical body, but his inmost being—himself, the *psyche*, the God-given soul!... It is man's creative and responsive soul which survives death. You cannot destroy the God-part! If a man possesses the breath or spirit of God, he will live [or continue to exist] on and on. He will never die."

E. Owen Crouch, in a volume of published letters to his daughter Lorna: "If man has been made in the image and likeness of God, then man is made for eternity, not time. There beats in the breast of every man immortality.... God has made man kin to the animal. Biologically we are 'dust of the earth,' hence animals. But eternity inhabits our hearts because we are 'like' God. To be truly and essentially human is to be divine, for we were made in the 'image and likeness' of God. And to be truly divine means to be *eternal*." "Constitutionally, man was *made to be* and *is* eternal in nature." "You are eternal, Lorna. God is in your heart." "Avoid subjecting your Godlike self to the husks of temporal needs." "Recognize the deity who is within you." Human nature "was made divine and to inherit eternity." [*Dear Lorna*, pp. 92-94]

F. John Clayton, a church of Christ writer who publishes a journal called *Does God Exist*, printed and defended these reflections from a 14-year old boy in the Sept/Oct 1996 issue: Our soul goes through three stages, says this lad. It existed before we were born, and then was placed in a fleshly body to be tested. For its third stage, "when the flesh dies, the soul escapes the flesh and accomplishes spiritual unity with the third realm. There it spends eternity.... The soul escapes the flesh when it dies and returns to where it came from.... A soul is a member of God. God, Christ, the Holy Spirit, and all our souls are one and the same and God takes parts of Himself and puts them in the flesh. Often those parts (souls) forget where they came from, forget who they are, and are caught up in the fleshly thoughts and feelings and lose touch with that much larger part of themselves. The body is only a tool that the soul uses to carry out his needs in the life." Our souls are "parts of God."

VII. Dottie Rambo, American gospel singer and songwriter, 1934-2008, wrote a song called "The Holy Hills." It says:

> *The holy hills of Heaven call me to*
> *mansions bright across the sea,*
> *Where loved ones wait and crowns are given*
> *when the hills of home start calling me.*
> *This house of clay is but a prison,*
> *bars of bone [that] hold my soul;*
> *But the doors of clay are gonna burst wide open*
> *when the angel sets my spirit free.*
> *I'll take my flight like a mighty eagle*
> *when the hills of home start calling me.*

THE ORIGIN OF HUMAN SOULS

QUESTION: In tonight's Bible study our minister said that God created for six days, then rested on the seventh day—never to create again. For me, this raises the question of the origin of each human soul. I know how my body got here, but my soul does not get here by reproduction. So, if God is not still creating, where has my soul been since day six of creation?

ANSWER: First, let us clarify what we mean by "soul." In the Bible the main words for the soul are Hebrew *nephesh* and Greek *psyche* (or *psuchē*). Each has three main uses: (1) the whole person as an individual; (b) the attribute of life (or "aliveness") as shared by all living things; and (c) the inner man or spiritual aspect (the spirit) of human beings. The Bible teaches that every human being has a soul in this third sense. Part of our essence as a human being, in addition to the body, is this soul (spirit, inner being).

The question asked here is this: where does the person's individual soul come from? What is its origin? This question has been debated down through Christian history, and outside of Christianity as well.

Outside of the context of Christianity, the most common view in western culture today is that there is no such thing as "the soul." This is the monistic view of human nature: we are bodies only. There is nothing to us besides the physical. Though quite a few "Christians" have accepted this monistic view under the influence of evolutionism, it is clearly anti-Biblical.

Another anti-Christian view is that somehow the individual soul of each person is eternal; it has existed forever in the past and will exist forever into the future, either as an individual entity or as a part of an undistinguished mass of "spirit." This view is typical of philosophical dualism, which says that physical stuff and spiritual stuff exist side by side in a dualism eternally; how the world of two-part human beings developed out of this is the product of various speculations. This view also derives from forms of pantheistic monism, such as classical Hinduism, which see individual souls as fallen bits of eternal spirit unfortunately separated from their ideal primal oneness. Both views are horribly pagan.

Christians who believe the Bible, on the other hand, down through the centuries have chosen between two main views of the origin of the individual soul. One view is called traducianism, which says that once Adam and Eve had been created with bodies and souls, *both* the body and the soul of any child were transmitted, passed along, or handed down from parents to child. The soul-substance is as much "inherited" or "reproduced" as the physical substance of the body.

This view was and is defended by major thinkers in Christian history, including Tertullian and possibly Augustine in the early church, and men such as W. G. T. Shedd, Millard Erickson, and Norman Geisler in more modern times. (Augustine was not sure, but seemed to lean in that direction because it made his view of original sin easier to defend.) Alexander Campbell seems to defend this view in chapter 7 of *The Christian System*, though he does not use the term. He says that it explains why children inherit their partially-depraved natures from their parents. He says, "Our nature was corrupted by the fall of Adam before it was transmitted to us; and hence that hereditary imbecility to do good, and that proneness to do evil, so universally apparent in all human beings" (Standard Publishing: n.d., p. 15).

The other view that has been widely accepted in Christendom is the creationist view, which says that each individual soul is created *ex nihilo* (from nothing) at the point of or shortly after the formation of the new human being in the mother's womb, and is united there with the new body. Men such as Jerome, Thomas Aquinas, John Calvin, Charles Hodge, and Louis Berkhof have defended this view.

This is also my personal view, but I do not spend a lot of time on this subject, for two reasons. One, there is not a clear explanation in the Bible of how individual souls originate. The arguments on each side (traducian and creationist) rest heavily on implication and speculation. Two, no other doctrines seem to be affected by the choice one makes here. Either view can be seen as consistent with other doctrines.

But this leads us to the question that was raised in the beginning above: is it true that "God rested on the seventh day—never to create again"? If so, then the creationist view of the origin of individual souls would not be possible. The truth is, however, that the text does NOT say – "never to create again"! All it says is that He rested from the task of initially creating the universe in its original form. This does not imply an absolute end to all works of creation.

The fact is that there have been other specific works of *ex nihilo* creation at points in world history, as needed, as recorded in Scripture. For example, on those occasions when God appeared in a theophany (e.g., a cloud, Exodus 13:21; Matthew 17:5; in human form with clothing, Genesis 18:1ff.; a dove, Luke 3:22), where did these forms come from? Where did they go when the theophany was completed? Most likely they were created from nothing, and then disappeared into nothing.

Also, most likely the new creation bodies the redeemed will receive at the second coming will actually be created from nothing, in a new kind of created stuff. And think of the five loaves and two fish—which miraculously multiplied into enough fishy material to feed thousands. Where did all that matter come from?

Likewise, it is reasonable to assume that each individual soul is created at the point of conception. So in answer to your question, your soul did not exist anywhere prior to your conception, when God brought it into existence from nothing.

SOUL AND SPIRIT: WHAT'S THE DIFFERENCE?

QUESTION: Can you explain to me the difference between soul and spirit? I know the word "soul" is used in different ways, and means life or living being; and I know we have a spirit by means of which we relate to God (in prayer, worship, etc.). I know that they are connected but are not the same—so what is the difference?

ANSWER: It is important first of all to distinguish between the WORDS "soul" (Hebrew, *nephesh*; Greek, *psychē*) and "spirit" (Hebrew, *ruach*; Greek, *pneuma*) on the one hand, and the metaphysical ENTITY or aspect of human nature to which these words apply, on the other hand.

In both the Old Testament and the New Testament the words translated "soul"—*nephesh* and *psychē*—have three major connotations, only one of which refers to the spiritual side of our metaphysical nature. First, in some contexts these words refer to the whole person or individual or self, and not to just one part of his or her nature. An Old Testament example is Genesis 2:7, which says that God's breathing into the nostrils of the clay figure was the means by which the latter became a living "*nephesh*," namely, a living individual or living *person*. The reference here is not to just one part of the person, but to the person as such. A New Testament example is Romans 13:1, which says that every "*psychē*" must be subject to governing authorities. Here the word applies to the whole *person*, not to any one part of the person.

A second connotation of the words usually translated "soul"—*nephesh* and *psychē*—is the characteristic or attribute of LIFE as such, as possessed by any living individual. This does not refer to the person as such, nor to any metaphysical part of the person; but to the life or livingness present in that person (or animal). See Leviticus 17:14; Matthew 6:25; John 10:11; 15:13.

The third connotation of these words is that the *nephesh* or *psychē* is an aspect of man's metaphysical nature, or part of the stuff out of which we are made. It applies to our *spiritual* nature, as distinct from our *physical* nature. E.g., Psalms 63:1 says, "My soul [*nephesh*] thirsts for you; my flesh faints for you" (ESV); see Psalms 84:2. This meaning is clearly seen in Matthew 10:28, "Do not fear those who kill the body but cannot kill the soul [*psychē*]. Rather fear him who can destroy both soul [*psychē*] and body in hell." Revelation 6:9 speaks of the souls [*psychē*] of martyrs who exist without their bodies in the angelic heaven in the presence of God.

Note carefully: neither of the first two connotations is relevant to our question here. We must be aware of them, however; and we must be careful to discern when these connotations are present so that we do not apply such verses to the metaphysical question. Many false theological conclusions have been drawn by applying texts where *nephesh* or *psychē* refers to the *PERSON* rather than to the *SPIRITUAL PART* of the person.

Now the question is this: what is the relation between the part of our nature called the SOUL in this third sense, and the part of our nature called the SPIRIT (e.g., Luke 23:46; Acts 7:59; 1 Corinthians 2:11; Hebrews 12:23)? Here is the bottom line: *they are the same thing; there is no distinction between them.* Human beings are made of two kinds of metaphysical stuff: physical and spiritual. The former is called "body," "flesh," and "outer man"; the latter is called "spirit," "soul," "heart," and "inner man." The soul IS the spirit. This view of man is called (anthropological) dualism, and sometimes dichotomy. It is the Biblical view.

It is commonly believed, though, that man is three parts (trichotomy), with the soul and the spirit being distinguished. I have concluded that this is false. The Bible overwhelmingly speaks of human beings as composed of two parts (see my book, *The Faith Once for All*, 138-140), and the same spiritual activities are applied to our spiritual nature whether it is called "soul" or "spirit." I.e., where "soul" and "spirit" are referring to a part of man's nature, they are synonymous and interchangeable. For example, both terms are used to refer to that part of man that survives death, i.e., the disembodied element in the intermediate state: soul (Matthew 10:28; Revelation 6:9; 20:4), spirit (Hebrews 12:23). Both terms are used for that part of man that departs at the moment of death: soul (Genesis 35:18; 1 Kings 17:21), spirit (Psalms 31:5; Luke 8:55; 23:46; Acts 7:59; James 2:26).

This interchangeability is also seen in the fact that the highest spiritual activities are experienced by a person, whether the seat of that experience is called the "soul" or the "spirit" (see John Murray, *Writings*, II:25-27). This is significant because for most trichotomists, man's spirit is supposed to be *the* seat of God-consciousness and spiritual experience (such as prayer and worship), with the soul being the seat of baser passions. But this distinction is not found in the Bible. For example, religious sorrow or spiritual grief is attributed to Jesus in His spirit (Mark 8:12; John 11:33; 13:21) and in His soul (Matthew 26:38; John 12:27). See Psalms 77:2-3. Also, in poetic parallelism Mary expresses spiritual joy and praise to God in both her soul and spirit (Luke 1:46-47). Contrary to the lower position trichotomy usually gives to the soul, the Bible pictures it as the subject of the highest exercises of devotion toward God. "At night my soul longs for You, indeed, my spirit within me seeks You diligently" (Isaiah 26:9). In Philippians 1:27 Paul exhorts us to stand firm in one spirit and strive together with one soul (*psychē*). Love for God, the highest virtue, comes from the soul (Mark 12:30). Hope is an anchor for the soul (Hebrews 6:19). We should obey God's will from the soul (*psychē*, Ephesians 6:6).

John Laidlaw says that such passages as these "render it impossible to hold that 'spirit' can mean exclusively or mainly the Godward side of man's inner nature, and 'soul' the rational or earthward. The terms are parallel, or practically equivalent, expressions for the inner life as contrasted with the outer or bodily life" (*The Biblical Doctrine of Man*, 90).

But what about the biblical passages that seem to teach trichotomy? These are actually very few (mainly Genesis 2:7; 1 Thessalonians 5:23; Hebrews 4:12), and may be readily understood in harmony with dualism (see *The Faith Once for All*, 141-142).

In recent theological discussion, the difference between dichotomy and trichotomy does not receive much attention, and I do not make a big deal of it since not much is at stake here. The biggest problem is that some people waste a lot of time combing Scripture for a perceived distinction between soul and spirit, and trying to apply this distinction to all sorts of human activities. The much bigger issue is the distinction between dichotomy or *dualism* on the one hand, and anthropological *monism* on the other. The tendency today, even among many evangelicals, is to deny the existence of a true spiritual aspect in human beings and to limit us to body only. This is a really serious false doctrine and must be vigorously opposed.

THE NATURE OF THE HUMAN CONSCIENCE

QUESTION: What is the conscience, and how does it work?

ANSWER: I have written on this in my commentary on Romans, as part of my comments on Romans 2:15, where Paul says that even pagans "show that the work of the law is written on their hearts, while their conscience also bears witness, and their conflicting thoughts accuse or even excuse them" (ESV). The following paragraphs are taken from this commentary (1996 ed., I:203-205).

The latter part of Romans 2:15 focuses on an innate aspect of human nature known as the conscience. The most important thing to know about the conscience is that it is *not* the same as "the work of the law written on the heart." The conscience itself has no content; it is not in itself a source of knowledge about right and wrong. It is rather an ability, a function. Specifically, conscience is the function of comparing our deeds with an accepted standard of morality, and of prodding us with a sense of guilt when a deed does not conform to the standard. It "examines and passes judgment on a man's conduct" (F. F. Bruce, *The Epistle of Paul to the Romans*, 1963:91). As Moses Lard says, "Conscience originates no truth. It merely approves conformity to truth, or to what is held as truth, and condemns violations of it" (*Commentary on Paul's Letter to Romans*, pp. 48-9). See Douglas Moo, *The Wycliffe Exegetical Commentary: Romans*, I:148.

Whether the conscience functions properly or not depends on the accuracy of the standard with which it compares our deeds. To the degree to which the image of God remains intact within any individual, the conscience will work as intended by God. To the degree that the law-content written on the heart has been corrupted, the conscience will malfunction. It is similar to a spelling-check computer program. The function of the program is to compare the user's word entries with a pre-established data base. Even if the program is functioning perfectly, it will not produce the right results if there are misspelled words in the data base. If the words in the original data base are correct, then the results can be trusted.

The only thing needed to make such a program more analogous to the conscience is an addition to the computer of a small handle the user can grip while the check is being made. If the word being checked is incorrect, the errant speller would receive a mild electrical shock. This would be equivalent to the "pangs" of conscience felt after doing wrong. This is how the conscience "bears witness" to the individual concerning the rightness of God's moral law, in addition to the witness of the internally-written law itself.

It is extremely important to remember this: wherever the knowledge of God's law has been corrupted, suppressed, exchanged, or in any way violated, the conscience will continue to function but will not produce trustworthy results. Until one has submitted to the saving work of Jesus Christ and the Holy Spirit, and has allowed the truth of Biblical revelation to reinform his original moral data base, the conscience will at times, perhaps most of the time, yield false results. World morality will continue at depravity level as long as "cricketology" prevails: "Always let your conscience be your guide" (cited from Jiminy Cricket). This is bad theology. Actually, the conscience itself *needs* a guide or standard, and the only sure guide for sinners is the objective Word of God, the Bible.

The last part of v. 15, in my opinion, is not different from the working of the conscience but is a clarification of how it works. The functioning conscience results in an inner dialogue, forcing the mind to verbalize thoughts such as "This must be OK," or "You know that's wrong, don't you?" Our thoughts either accuse us or defend us in reference to our deeds. These are technical legal terms that suggest a courtroom trial where the individual is the defendant and his own conscience-driven thoughts are both the prosecuting attorney and the defense lawyer.

This inner witness or testimony occurs day by day, and not just at the final judgment. Also, the accusing or defending happens with reference to individual deeds, and not to anyone's life as a whole. Thus Paul is not saying that on the day of judgment there may be some Gentile whose conscience will excuse him altogether so that he is saved. This is definitely not Paul's point. He is saying only that sometimes in this life, when a Gentile does by nature what the law requires in a certain situation, his conscience will excuse him regarding that one decision. Paul hints that this is the exception rather than the rule, however, since he says their thoughts will accuse them or *even* defend them, as if the latter is unexpected.

When this inner moral consciousness (the inwardly-written law plus the conscience) is combined with the knowledge of God learned through the created universe (Romans 1:18-21), the result is that even the Gentiles know that this law is the law of the Creator-God and that they are guilty before God when they break it and are worthy of the wrath God has ordained for such lawbreakers (see 1:32).

SECTION THREE

SIN

WILL WE HAVE FREE WILL IN HEAVEN?

QUESTION: Will we have free will in heaven? If we will not be able to sin, how can we say we will have free will?

ANSWER: The common assumption here is that a *certain kind* of free will is part of the essence of humanness. To begin with, the free will assumed here is the ability to choose between opposites; in fact, free will is often defined simply as "the power of opposite choice." It is called "free" will because we can make that choice between opposites without that choice's being fixed or determined by some power outside our own will.

When we dig a little deeper into the problem, though, we will see that the most common assumption is that true free will is actually the power of opposite *moral* choice; i.e., it includes the ability to choose between good and evil, or the ability to choose to sin or not to sin. Based on Biblical teaching about human existence in this world, we must say that human beings do indeed have such free will in this earthly life. But is that the whole story about free will?

At this point I will raise a question that I do not think has been given enough attention: does the fact that human beings have such free will in this earthly life require that we must *always* have it in order to be fully human? Is such free will truly part of the *essence* of humanness? This is sometimes just taken for granted, and this assumption gives rise to the above questions. But here I choose to use my own free will (!) to challenge this assumption. I regard this kind of free will to be a necessary aspect of our EARTHLY life as human beings. It is part of the nature of our earthly life as a probationary period, with the choices we make during this segment of our existence determining whether or not we are eternally saved or lost. But this does not require that human beings must ALWAYS have free will, *in the sense described above.*

The reason I say, "in the sense described above," is that it is just *assumed* that the power of opposite choice must include, or be understood as, the power of opposite *moral* choice. This is a point I am challenging. We can have the power to choose between opposites (including yes-or-no decisions) without there being any moral implications involved. We can also have the power to choose simply between different options on matters that have no moral implications. In order to make this point clear, I will suggest that we use another summary description of free will as it will apply in heaven. Since it will still be the power to choose between various options, I am thinking that we could call it "the power of optional choice." Also, we could just call it "the power of different choice." All the powers of choosing, or of making decisions between options, would still be present, except for that one element that has application only during our life on this earth.

Thus in answer to the question above, the saved in heaven will indeed have freedom, but not free will in the sense of being able to choose to sin. When God perfects the saints (at death, even before the final heaven—Hebrews 12:23), and confirms them in their holiness, they will no longer be able to sin. We will be confirmed in holiness as free creatures who have already demonstrated (by our free acts) our preference and desire for that state. In our final state we will be as spiritually pure and beautiful as a holy bride dressed for her wedding (Revelation 19:8). We will live forever in a completely glorified state, unable to sin again. But we will be fully human, and will still have true freedom. In fact, we will never have been MORE human, or MORE free.

Let me summarize these two different forms or aspects of free will. One is the "power of opposite choice," in the sense of "the power of opposite moral choice"; the other is the "power of different choice." The libertarian concept of free will is usually identified with the former, or seen as having to include the former. I am saying this is not a *necessary* aspect of free will. The will is still free as long as it has the ability to choose among various options, even where there are no accompanying moral implications. It is simply the freedom to select one course of action from a list of many possible choices.

I would also suggest that this is the kind of free will that God has. God's freedom is a true freedom even though His nature does not allow Him to choose to do evil. God is not free in the sense of being able to choose between moral opposites, but He is free in the significant sense of being able to choose among an infinite number of possibilities in regard to what He decides to do.

So how does the two-fold nature of free will apply to us as human beings? In summary, we are designed to experience *both* kinds of freedom outlined above. In this lifetime we possess both the ability to choose between moral opposites *and* the ability to choose among different options. Both are true freedoms, with the former being what most people call "libertarian" freedom. This power of opposite choice is necessary during this lifetime, because this period of our existence is a kind of "trial period," a time of probation, as it were, which will determine our eternal status. This aspect of our freedom has no parallel in God's nature, but was probably also the condition of angels in their initially-created existence (which was also probably a probation period, ending after the event described in 2 Peter 2:4).

Once we die, our freedom of opposite moral choice will be removed from our nature, and from that point on we will possess only the ability to choose among different options, exactly after the pattern of God's freedom (except our choices will always be finite). We will no longer be able to sin, having been perfected in our sanctification and having been truly made holy as God is holy (Hebrews 12:23; 1 Peter 1:16).

THE AWFULNESS OF SIN

PART ONE: SIN DEVASTATES GOD

My wife, Barbara, has remarked many times how she wishes that we had kept a diary of all the places where I have spoken, along with the record of the sermons and lessons I have given, over the sixty years of my ministry. If I had done this, I would be able to tell you exactly when and where this following sermon series on "The Awfulness of Sin" was delivered. But such a record was not kept, so all I can tell you is that this series was given in the late twentieth century, somewhere in Prince Edward Island, Canada. I don't think I have used it anywhere else. Maybe that is because the subject of sin is not very popular.

After I wrote the above introduction to this sermon series, and just before finishing this book, I found the data concerning how this sermon series originated! See that data in the general Preface pages ii-iii above.

INTRODUCTION

"Against Thee, Thee only, I have sinned,
And done what is evil in Thy sight."
— Psalms 51:4a

In today's world, people do not like the word "sin." You can speak about law-breaking, wrong-doing, crime, error, anti-social behavior, short-comings, corruption, irresponsibility, selfishness, misdeeds, vice, even *evil*. But don't call it *sin*! Why not? Because "sin" has unmistakable *religious* overtones, conjuring up the face of GOD, and the law of GOD. It suggests that our negative behavior is in a real sense a violation of the law of *God*. And the one thing modern man does not want to do is to think that his behavior has anything to do with God.

Even if we use the word "sin," for most people it is not sin against *God*. In our time you can sin against animals; you can sin against trees; you can sin against the environment as such; you can sin against yourself; you can sin against other individuals or groups of individuals (the poor, women, children); you can sin against races of people—but not against GOD!

Here's the deal – sin really is not *sin* unless it is understood as a *violation of the laws of the Creator*. Sin is not sin unless it is sin against *God*. As the Psalmist David says, "Against Thee, Thee only, I have sinned." This is the most important thing I can tell you about the awfulness of sin: it is sin *against God!* In fact, sin *devastates* God.

The whole idea that something we human beings do can affect God *in any way* has been widely denied. For example, representatives of the pagan philosophy called Epicureanism (see Acts 17:18) did not all agree that any gods exist at all, but those who said they do exist thought of them as having no contact whatsoever with our world. As one writer put it, for the Epicureans "the gods are completely separate from the rest of reality; they are uninterested in it, play no role in it, and remain completely undisturbed by it."

A similar view is present sometimes within the boundaries of Christendom. In fact, a main doctrine of classical Calvinism is that the sovereign God *never reacts* and *never responds* to anything outside Himself. Whatever happens does so because God predetermines it and then causes it. I have summed this Calvinist view up in the statement, "God always acts; He never reacts." This applies to everything, including sin itself. I call this aspect of Calvinism the principle of *unconditionality*. I.e., Calvinists cannot bring themselves to admit that *anything* in God's experience can be conditioned by man or can be a reaction to something in the creation. (See my treatment of this in my book, *What the Bible Says About God the Ruler* [College Press, 1984], chapter 5, "Special Providence and Free Will.")

Such an idea is quite false, however. God interacts with human beings and responds to our actions because that is the way He sovereignly chose to make us, i.e., with free will. This is an aspect of the self-limitation under which God chose to relate to us when He decided to create us with relative independence. Our free-will choices affect God in many ways, and nothing affects Him more than our sin. In fact, our sin has a profound effect upon God. It *devastates* Him; it tears Him apart; it cuts Him to the heart.

We can affirm without hesitation that sin cause God untold *pain*. (See my book, *What the Bible Says About God the Redeemer* [College Press, 1984], pp. 509-520.) We have superstitions about such things on a human level. In occult circles people jab voodoo dolls with pins, thinking it causes pain in others. When walking down a sidewalk, children used to cite the rhyme, "Step on a crack, break your grandmother's back." The fact is that many of the things we do cause great pain and anguish for loved ones—see the devastation caused by unfaithful spouses, drunken parents, and disobedient children.

When I was a boy and had disobeyed my parents, I knew that I was causing them heartache. I could see the pain in my mother's eyes. This is no less true in our relation to God. We cannot see God's "eyes" and the pain in them, but the fact is this: our every sin causes Him pain! Sin is a wound in the heart of God!

Some Christian theologians have decided that God is so unchangeable (immutable) that he simply cannot suffer in any sense. They call this God's "impassibility" (from a Latin word meaning "to suffer"). This is wrong! Genesis 6:6 (NIV, 1978) declares, "The LORD was grieved that he had made man on the earth, and his heart was filled with pain." As the NASB puts it, "He was grieved in His heart." In Jeremiah 31:20 God says this: "Is Ephraim my dear son? Is he a delightful child? Indeed, as often as I have spoken against him, I certainly still remember him, therefore **my heart yearns** for him." This lament of God literally says at the end, "My bowels (stomach) *moan/groan/ache* for him." Isaiah 63:10 says, "They rebelled, and grieved His Holy Spirit" (see Ephesians 4:30). And Luke 19:41 says of Jesus, "And when He approached, He saw the city, and wept over it."

Here we see the *awfulness* of sin, and how it causes infinite pain in the heart of God. From this point on I will explain two ways in which sin causes agony in God.

I. SIN VIOLATES THE *LOVE* OF GOD

Sin devastates God simply because He is the kind of God that He is. We are all familiar with what 1 John 4:8 affirms, namely, "God is love." God *loves* us. And when we sin against God, we sin against His love for us.

If God were any other kind of God, sin might not be so awful, at least from God's standpoint. If God did not love us so much, maybe sin would not be so bad. The fact is that the Biblical concept of God is unique in revealing Him to us as a God of love. No other concepts of God, those based on human imagination and speculation, portray the deity as a loving being. One theologian says that love as a divine attribute is "the Christian specialty." Another says that the affirmation "God is love" would sound hollow if we tried to apply it to other so-called deities of the world. (Emil Brunner, *The Christian Doctrine of God: Dogmatics, Vol. I* [Westminster: 1950], p. 183).

To say that sin would hurt a non-loving god simply would not make sense. In stories and movies, rebellion against a bully, or a heartless tyrant (e.g., Adolf Hitler, Pol Pot, Saddam Hussein) is looked at as a noble act. And so also, if the deity were mean and heartless, it might even be admirable to sin and rebel against him.

But He is not this kind of deity. The God of the Bible, the true God, is a loving Father who lavishes His goodness upon us and wants to bless us with all the blessings His power and glory can muster. We are His children, whom He wants to embrace close to His heart. Thus when we sin, we are rebelling against His *love*, injuring and wounding Him in His heart. Every sin is like a slap in the face of the God who *loves* you!

This is why sin devastates God. Whenever anyone is rejected by someone he or she loves, pain is inevitable. See this picture God draws of Himself in relation to rebellious Israel: "I permitted Myself to be sought by those who did not ask for Me; I permitted Myself to be found by those who did not seek Me. I said, 'Here am I, here am I,' to a nation which did not call on My name. I have spread out My hands all day long to a rebellious people, who walk in the way which is not good, following their own thoughts." You can imagine the tears running down God's face as He recites these words!

You can see these same tears on Jesus's face when he says this about His people Israel: "Jerusalem, Jerusalem, who kills the prophets and stones those who are sent to her! How often I wanted to gather your children together, the way a hen gathers her chicks under her wings, and you were unwilling" (Matthew 23:37) In another place Jesus is specifically said to weep over the holy city (Luke 19:41).

Often we wonder why we sin, and we wonder how we could ever reach some mental state where we could just automatically say "NO!" to temptation. What thoughts can be so powerful that they can motivate us to resist sin and yield in obedience to God? Jesus said it best: "If you love Me, you will keep My commandments" (John 14:15). Why is this? Because if we love Him, we will *not want to hurt Him!* This is why we must fully grasp this concept that *sin devastates God!* How can we bear to hurt the one we love?

When I was a young boy, I found some books in my Grandma Mitchell's house that I just devoured. One was Robin Hood; I could not bear it when in the end Robin shot an arrow as far away as he could and instructed his followers to bury him where it landed. "And there they buried bold Robin Hood." So sad!

But another book was even harder to put down: *Little Men*, by Louisa May Alcott. The opening line is, "Please, sir, is this Plumfield?" This was spoken by a desperate lad seeking a home in the orphanage for boys by that name, run by Jo (one of Alcott's *Little Women*) and her husband, the kind Mr. Bhaer. Nat was accepted, and he fit in well at Plumfield. He was a good boy, and he loved Mr. and Mrs. Bhaer very much. But he had one character problem: he lied at times. Mr. Bhaer reprimanded him for it, and told him that if he did it again, he would go through a difficult punishment process.

The inevitable happened: Nat got in a tough spot and lied again, and Mr. Bhaer heard about it and summoned the penitent Nat into the school for his punishment. One of the other boys, Tommy, was peeking through a window and saw Mr. Bhaer take down a big ruler. "Yikes!" he said; "Nat's going to get it now."

But this is what he saw. Mr. Bhaer asks Nat if he is ready for his punishment. The teary Nat tries to beg off, but this was not going to happen. Then, instead of asking Nat to hold out his hand and accept the blows to his palm, Mr. Bhaer hands the ruler to Nat and *holds out his own palm*, and tells Nat, "This is your punishment: you have to hit my hand six times very hard with the ruler." Nat is crying now and says he just can't do it—because he really, truly *loved* Mr. Bhaer and did not want to hurt him! But the teacher insisted; so Nat gave him a couple of little taps. "Harder!" says Mr. Bhaer. Finally the sobbing Nat finishes, throws the ruler away across the room, "and hugging the kind hand in both his own, laid his face down on it sobbing out of a passion of love, and shame, and penitence."

Nat had learned his lesson the hard way: we should do everything we can to avoid hurting the one we love.

II. SIN EVOKES THE *WRATH* OF GOD

The second way sin devastates God is that it forces Him to express an attribute that He would rather let lie dormant, i.e., it causes His holy nature to take on the form of *wrath* in order to punish the sin.

Wrath is a side of God's nature that most people want to deny and forget about, and we can understand why. The fact is that wrath is a side of God's nature that would never have been openly displayed if *sin* had never entered the picture. But once sin has been brought into existence by free-will creatures, God has no choice but to *oppose* it in His wrath. His righteous and holy nature requires it. Just as God is love, and must be true to his loving nature, so also God is holy wrath—"Our God is a consuming fire" (Hebrews 12:29), and He must be true to this side of His nature also.

To say that this "must be true" of God's nature brings to mind Ray Bradbury's science-fiction story titled "451 Degrees Fahrenheit." This is the (approximate) temperature at which paper spontaneously bursts into flames. I.e., it is the very nature of paper to be consumed by fire once it reaches that temperature, e.g., in an oven. By analogy, sin is like paper, and God's nature is such that his holy wrath will ultimately consume it. That is simply who He is. As Nahum 1:6 says, "Who can stand before His indignation? Who can endure the burning of His anger? His wrath is poured out like fire and the rocks are broken up by Him."

Jonathan Edwards is famous not only for his theology as such but also for a sermon that he first preached in 1741, "Sinners in the Hands of an Angry God." His basic Scripture text was Deuteronomy 32:35, "It is mine to avenge; I will repay. In due time their foot will slip; their day of disaster is near and their doom rushes upon them" (NIV). This portrayal of an "angry God" is not softened in the New Testament. In Hebrews 10:26ff. we read, "For if we go on sinning willfully after receiving the knowledge of the truth, there no longer remains a sacrifice for sins, but a terrifying expectation of judgment and the fury of a fire which will consume the adversaries…. For we know Him who said, 'Vengeance is Mine, I will repay.' And again, 'The Lord will judge His people.' It is a terrifying thing to fall into the hands of the living God."

The ultimate expression of God's wrath is hell itself—the Lake of Fire (Revelation 20:14-15; 21:8). Hell is by no means an expression of God's love; this is a serious and grievous error I have seen asserted by some

Christian preachers. I have little sympathy for those who want to weaken the doctrine of eternal hell, and diminish the intensity of God's wrath.

But my point here is not to explore how sinners must suffer the torments of hell as the result of their sins, but to emphasize the fact that sin devastates *God Himself!* We have seen how sin violates God's love, and causes Him inward pain as a loving God. But here we are talking about His wrath. Is it possible that when sin evokes the wrath of God, this also causes God Himself a kind of inward agony and pain? The answer is YES – because, when God pours out His fiery wrath upon sin, He is doing the very opposite of what he WANTS to do in His heart of hearts.

Do not misunderstand. Wrath is a natural aspect of God's holy nature. This is *who He is!* But even though it is God's nature to consume sin and sinners in the fire of His wrath, this does not mean that he *likes* to do it or *wants* to do it. Remember: God is both love and wrath at the same time! (See Romans 11:22.) If He were *only* wrath, or *only* love, there would be no pain in his heart in the presence of sin. If He were wrath only, He could just condemn everyone to hell—and good riddance! Or if He were love only, He could just save everybody and forget about the punishment.

But God is both, and this means He is *torn* between the two responses to sin that are required by His very nature: He *wants to save* the very ones whom He *has to punish* in eternal hell! God is "not wishing for any to perish but for all to come to repentance" (2 Peter 3:9). "For He does not afflict willingly" (Lamentations 3:33). The literal reading of this verse is, "For He does not afflict *from His heart.*" When God does necessary things as the expression of His wrath, this is His "strange work," His "alien task," says Isaiah 28:21 (NIV).

And what is it that calls forth and requires this "strange work" of God? What makes it necessary for His holy nature to burst forth in fiery wrath? What forces this pain, this devastation upon God Himself? WE DO! When we SIN!

What pain can be greater than having to punish someone you love with all your heart? Sometimes we present a caricature of a parent who is spanking a child while saying "This hurts me more than it hurts you!" ("Yeah, sure!" the wincing child is thinking sarcastically.) But extend this scene into infinity, and you will get some idea of the pain we cause God when *we* sin against *Him*—especially if we remain unsaved and must be sent to hell. For God Himself, this is the opposite of what His love desires—it is *devastating pain* in His heart.

How does God deal with this terrible tension within Himself, this agony caused by our sin. He has already done what He can—through the cross of Jesus Christ (which will be discussed in part four, below). But some of this pain will remain within God's heart forever, since many will perish and not come to repentance.

CONCLUSION

What can we ourselves do to ease this pain in God's heart? We must stop thinking of our sins in the abstract. We must start thinking of them one by one—and of what they are doing *to God*. Maybe then we will have a "River Kwai" experience: "What have I done—*to God*?"

Let's remember that what we do, *does affect God*. Yes, we cause Him pain when we sin. But the opposite is true also! We don't have to cause Him pain—we can cause Him JOY instead! This is what happens when an unsaved sinner repents and turns to God for salvation! Luke 17:10 says that "there is joy in the presence of the angels of God over one sinner who repents." This does not specifically say that the angels themselves are rejoicing—though I am sure this is true. But what it actually says is that there is joy *in the presence of* the angels when a sinner repents. And who is in the presence of the angels? (See Revelation 4 & 5.) The answer is: *God Himself!* If you are not a Christian, you can cause joy in the heart of God by turning your life over to Him and obeying the gospel!

THE AWFULNESS OF SIN

PART TWO: SIN DESTROYS MAN

INTRODUCTION

"The person who sins will die." — Ezekiel 18:4b

God spent the first five days of creation preparing the universe that would become the home of the human race (Genesis 1:1-25). At each step along the way, "God saw that it was good." Then on the sixth day He created human beings—Adam and Eve—as the "crown of creation." After this climactic bit of handiwork, "behold, it was **very** good" (Genesis 1:31). Speaking to God about mankind, David, the inspired psalmist, says, "You have made him a little lower than God ['*Elohīm*]" (Psalms 8:5).

When we look out over the world of humanity as it exists today, we do indeed see many great achievements and advancements. We can say alongside Jimmy Stuart, "It's a wonderful life!" – or sing along with Louis Armstrong, "What a wonderful world!"

But when you look at man and his world more closely, you can see that it is not as wonderful as it seems at first glance. Even in the natural world, many things we take for granted as normal, such as destructive tsunamis and hurricanes, are not. Especially in the interpersonal world of human beings, we can see that it is filled with cheating, selfishness, greed, injustice, abuse, warfare, and violence of all kinds—in other words, it is filled with the overall rot and decay and destruction of *sin*.

Many decades ago, I listened on some form of broadcasting (probably radio) to a debate between two college debate teams. The resolution being debated was this: "Man, all things considered, is a disappointment." The positive team, arguing that the human race is indeed a disappointment, cited as evidence the existence of war, poverty, and hatred. They did a good job covering the evidence, but what intrigued me was the idea that, even in view of such things as these, man is *just* a "disappointment"—rather than a tragedy or a disaster. The negative team was struggling to present our race is such a positive light that we cannot be considered even a *disappointment*!

My thesis here is that, despite some very great accomplishments over the centuries, the sinful human race is overall in a state of disaster and disarray, yea, even destruction. The evidence for this is the universal presence of sin, and the fact that sin destroys those who are under its power. In this lesson I will explain how this is the case.

I. SIN DESTROYS OUR RELATIONSHIP WITH GOD

First, sin destroys our relationship with God. We see this in the Garden of Eden itself. Adam and Eve began human existence in a most blessed state, not just because they were in a physical paradise, but because they had a close positive relationship with their Creator-God. The fact that they recognized the "sound of the LORD God walking in the garden" (Genesis 3:8) implies that this contact between them and God had already been occurring on a regular basis. They lived in friendship, fellowship, harmony, and peace with God.

But sin destroyed that kind of relationship! This happened not just for Adam and Eve, but for all their offspring that would follow, including ourselves. No more personal interaction with a theophany (visible presence) of God! That kind of relationship has been destroyed for as long as we live upon this earth, especially as unsaved sinners. Now, because of that destroyed relationship with God, the unsaved sinner can be described as desolate, detested, and damned to hell.

DESOLATE. Even though He is our Creator, sin separates us from the very God in whose image we were made. The sinner is alone, forsaken, disowned, divorced, deserted, cut off from God's presence. This is actually a double desolation. First, the sinner feels the need to *hide from God*. This was the first impulse of the sinful pair in Eden when they heard the Creator's footsteps: they "hid themselves from the presence of the LORD God" (Genesis 3:8). Sinners still try to hide from God by suppressing their knowledge of His presence all around them (Romans 1:18) and denying His very existence.

Second, sinners sink into desolation because *God turns away from them*. Once God had pronounced sentence upon Adam and Eve, He drove them out of the Garden of Eden, away from the place of His presence with them (Genesis 3:24). Sinners have become God's enemies (Romans 5:10). "Whoever wishes to be a friend of the world makes himself an enemy of God" (James 4:4). As Isaiah 59:2 explains, "But your iniquities have made a separation between you and your God, and your sins have hidden His face from you so that He does not hear." "Behold, I am against you," God said to sinful Israel (Jeremiah 50:31; Ezekiel 21:3). "The face of the Lord is against those who do evil" (1 Peter 3:12).

DETESTED. As if being desolate and forsaken by God were not bad enough, we also learn that God *detests* sinners. We often hear it said, "God hates sin but loves the sinner." This much is true, but it is not the whole story. God does love the sinner, since His nature is love. But remember: God's nature is also the *consuming fire of holy wrath*. And the Bible specifically says that God *hates* or detests sinners. This sums up God's personal relationship with the sinner.

This is clearly stated in Psalms 5:5-6, "You hate all who do iniquity. You destroy those who speak falsehood; the LORD abhors the man of bloodshed and deceit." "The one who loves violence His soul hates" (Psalms 11:5). Proverbs 6:16-19 lists seven things God hates, including "a false witness who utters lies, and one who spreads strife among brothers." God also hates "the perverse in heart" (Proverbs 11:20) and "everyone who is proud" (Proverbs 16:5). There were times when God said of Israel, "Therefore I have come to hate her" (Jeremiah 12:5; see Psalms 78:59; Hosea 9:15).

DAMNED. Desolate and detested by God in this life, the sinner's eternal fate is even worse. The sinner stands damned to hell, which is a state of eternal, unreconcilable separation from God. Jesus speaks these words to the damned on Judgment Day: "I never knew you; depart from Me, you who practice lawlessness" (Matthew 7:23); and, "Depart from Me, accursed ones" (Matthew 25:41). Sinners "will pay the penalty of eternal destruction, away from the presence of the Lord and from the glory of His power" (2 Thessalonians 1:9).

Being a sinner is like being in debt to God. Praying for forgiveness is praying for God to forgive our debts (Matthew 6:16). We have broken His law; we owe Him the debt of eternal punishment in hell. To die unforgiven is to be put to work so as to pay off that debt. The only problem is that it is an *eternal* sentence; we will never be able to finish paying what we owe. In a parable Jesus told, He said thinking your time in hell will ever come to an end is like a man living now who owes a king 150,000 *years'* wages (Matthew 18:23-35, especially v. 24). The situation of the damned is hopeless.

Why, then, is sin so awful? For one thing, it destroys the sinner's relationship with God. The sinner is desolate in His separation from God, detested by God, and damned to eternal separation from God.

II. SIN DESTROYS OUR RELATIONSHIP WITH THE WORLD

Something we learn from Genesis 3 is that sin destroys the integrity of the physical universe in which we live, and it destroys our intended relationship with that universe. When Paul reflects on this in Romans 8, he describes the personified world thus: "For we know that the whole creation groans and suffers the pains of childbirth together until now" (8:22). Using the curse upon womanhood consisting of pain in childbirth (Genesis 3:16) as an analogy, he says that this kind of disruption and suffering has affected the entire universe as the result of Adam and Eve's sin.

DISRUPTED. Because of sin, the relationship God originally intended between human beings and the rest of this physical creation is now destroyed. The original roles to be filled by man and his environment are summed up in God's pronouncements regarding Adam and Eve in Genesis 1:26-28. Here He says they are created to "rule over" the animal kingdom and "subdue" the entire earth. The creation around us is supposed to be our servant, and we are supposed to use it for the good of mankind and for the glory of God. Speaking of mankind, Psalms 8:6 says to God, "You make him to rule over the works of Your hands; You have put all things under his feet."

But now that we have become sinners, this relationship is disrupted. It is actually a part of the curse that God has placed upon the world as punishment for the sin of the First Pair. He said to them in Genesis 3:17-19, "Cursed is the ground because of you; in toil you will eat of it all the days of your life. Both thorns and thistles it shall grow for you; and you will eat the plants of the field; by the sweat of your face you will eat bread, till you return to the ground." This makes us ponder the question, "Who is really subduing whom in this man-world relationship?"

Instead of yielding easily to human labor, the universe now resists us and fights against us. Man in return fights back, and selfishly exploits and abuses the good bounties of the world. To use an appropriate environmental analogy, we have "fouled our own nest."

DECAYING. We can also say that sin has introduced an unnatural element of decay into our universe. We learn this from Paul's description of the fallen universe in Romans 8:21, where he says that the creation itself is looking ahead and longing for the time when it "will be set free from its slavery to corruption." Another familiar translation of that last phrase is "bondage to decay" (e.g., NIV, NRSV).

This is not referring to what is obviously the localized and natural decaying processes of organic materials like leaves and wood and waste products. So what kind of decay is introduced into the world because of sin? It is possible that this way of describing the curse brought upon the world because of sin includes the pollution and destruction of our environment through such selfish human practices as deforestation, over-harvesting, and pollution of the seas with plastic. It also might refer to a kind of cosmic decay, suggesting that the law of entropy (the universe is "running down") is not a natural state of things but was introduced as part of the curse upon the whole creation.

DISTORTED. The last way sin is destroying the universe is that the processes we think of as "natural," i.e., governed by the laws of nature, are not always normal in terms of God's original purpose for the natural world. I am not saying that the world was never intended to experience lightning storms, flooded plains, or high winds. But the so-called "natural disasters" (an oxymoron?), i.e., the kinds that destroy human life and possessions, are most probably a result of the curse put on the physical world as the result of sin.

We have got used to accepting such things as killer tornadoes, hurricanes, volcanic eruptions, and tsunamis; we have long said, "That's just the way things are." We have even been conditioned to believe the falsehood, "Whatever is, is good." It is true, though, that in recent times we have begun to blame human-originated "global warming" or "climate change" for an intensification of these phenomena; and there may be some truth to that. But even if that is so, it only illustrates the fact that the destructive elements in our environment are the result of human sin—Adam's, if not modern man's.

I am very comfortable in saying that sin has *distorted* our world, so that it is now a mixture of created nature's rich blessings and occasional natural disasters, and it is not always easy to tell which is which. The

Creator is indeed a loving God who "richly supplies us with all things to enjoy" (1 Timothy 6:17). The universe bears witness to the glory of God (Psalms 19:1), and the truth about God's power and love is clearly known by observing the world we live in (Romans 1:19-20). "He did not leave Himself without witness, in that He did good and gave you rains from heaven and fruitful seasons, satisfying your hearts with food and gladness" (Acts 14:17). But I think we have to say that this testimony is somewhat distorted by the presence of what are called "natural evils" and "natural disasters" mixed in with the good and satisfying things. What makes it all bearable is knowing that the negative phenomena are not God's original purpose; they are here because of human sin.

III. SIN DESTROYS OUR BODIES

Human beings are dualistic in the sense that each person has both a physical body and a spiritual soul. The latter is sometimes called the spirit, or the heart, or the inner man. Sin affects both sides of our nature. Here we will see how sin has destroyed our bodies in three ways: our bodies are dead, diseased, and dominated by sin.

DEAD. Even before Adam sinned, God warned him that he and Eve must not eat from the tree of knowledge of good and evil, "for in the day that you eat from it you will surely die" (Genesis 2:17). When they disobeyed and ate from it, God pronounced the curse of death upon them: "For you are dust, and to dust you shall return" (Genesis 3:21). Because of Adam's unique role as representative for all of his future offspring, this curse has been passed along to the whole human race. "Therefore, just as through one man sin entered into the world, and death through sin, and so death spread to all men, because all sinned" (Romans 5:12). Thus even from the moment of conception, we are existing in a body that has already been destroyed by sin. As Paul says in Romans 8:10, "The body is dead because of sin."

The false doctrine of biological evolutionism has caused countless individuals to reject this teaching that death is not natural to the human race. Under the influence of Darwin, they have accepted the lie that death is as natural as life itself. We must fight against this lie. Nothing is more *unnatural* than a funeral, or a cemetery. When Jesus went to the tomb of His friend Lazarus shortly after the latter's death, John 11:35 says that He wept. These were not just tears of sorrow, but tears of *rage*. In verse 33 the Greek word translated "deeply moved" has the sense of snorting with anger and displeasure. Biblical scholar B. B. Warfield says that Jesus was here feeling rage and fury against the enemy death that had caused so much sorrow and suffering for his friends. On death as an enemy, see 1 Corinthians 15:26.

DISEASED. The curse of death upon the human body does not strike us in just the single blow that ends our lives on this earth. Death has already begun to affect bodily form and functions from the moment of conception. Many children begin their existence with genetic abnormalities and brain malformations and other kinds of birth defects. All our lives we are the targets of bacteria and viruses that infect us with an unbelievable spectrum of diseases, each with its own specialty as to bodily location and function. Everything from the "common cold" to catastrophic cancer is just another step toward that conclusive calamity of death.

DOMINATED. To say that our bodies are dominated by sin is not a familiar way of speaking for most of us. Christian theology has always recognized that sin has caused severe negative physical consequences for our bodies, but we have not focused much on the spiritual effects of sin upon them. I never thought about it myself until I was writing my commentary on Romans (which was published in two volumes by College Press in 1996 and 1998). Up to that time I had accepted the common idea that when the apostolic writings refer to "the flesh" as something sinful, they are referring not to the body but to the old, pre-Christian way of life, i.e., not to an entity but to a state.

I changed my mind when I was working my way carefully through Paul's teaching in Romans 6 through 8. In these chapters I realized that

Paul is teaching not only that the soul has been corrupted by sin, but also that the body has been invaded by and colonized by sin. This is something quite different from the physical consequences of sin on the body, i.e., death and disease. Paul is telling us that the power of sin has a spiritual presence in our bodies, that sinful inclinations indwell our bodies and attempt to exert a constant influence upon our spirits. This is why he calls it "the body of sin" in Romans 6:6 (as more literally translated in the New English Translation): "We know that our old man was crucified with him so that the body of sin would no longer dominate us, so that we would no longer be enslaved to sin." I.e., the body itself is "depraved," infused with sin, infected with sin, distorted with weaknesses toward evil. This is not true because of its *nature* as physical; it is the result of the power of sin.

Modern sinners seek desperately to find genetic, or hormonal, or brain-originated origins for behavior considered to be sinful in Scripture, e.g., homosexualism, alcoholism, violence. Such possibilities are widely debated. But even if such evidence is found in unusual physical arrangements in some folks' genes or brains, this does not excuse such behavior and does not mean that such inclinations are "normal." If such a presence is found, this must be regarded as a part of the effects of sin upon human individuals, parallel to the way we view all genetic and birth defects in light of Romans 8:18-23.

This may also help us to understand the whole phenomenon of *addiction* toward substances and practices related to the body. This would include addiction for alcohol, nicotine, drugs, food, and sex. We have to recognize that the body is not just some inert and neutral entity; it is a sin-dominated part of our existence. It is not working right, because it is dominated by sin!

Romans 6:6 actually speaks of one of the great blessings of the salvation God bestows upon us when we obey the gospel. The whole point of this verse as quoted above is that in our baptism (see vv. 1-5) our *spirits* (the "old man" or "old self") were changed in the act of regeneration by the Holy Spirit, but our bodies were not. Our spirits which were dead in sin are here raised from that spiritual death into new life. We were born again, infused with "power from on high." And one of the results of that event is this: "so that the body of sin would no longer dominate us"! Most translations get this wrong, and say things like "might be destroyed" or "might be done away with." But Paul is talking about our physical bodies; they are not destroyed or done away with in baptism. Nor, unfortunately, are our "bodies of sin" cleansed from that indwelling sin presence in our baptism. In fact, in that moment we are only "half-saved"—our spirits are saved, but not our bodies. The sin presence is still in our bodies, BUT— here is the main point—our spirits have been given new strength so that we are now ABLE to keep these bodies under control!

This is important: this sin-presence in the body never has been and is not now an *excuse* for any kind of sin. So we now understand that one of our main sanctification responsibilities is this: "Do not let sin reign **in your mortal body** that you should obey its lusts, and do not go on presenting **the members of your body** to sin as instruments of unrighteousness" (Romans 6:12-13)! You now CAN control your body, so DO IT! Paul laments the fact that he still has to fight this battle with his body, and often loses (Romans 7:14ff.). But he relies on Christ and the indwelling Holy Spirit for the power to get better and better at it (Romans 7:24ff., especially 8:12-13). We understand now why he says in 1 Corinthians 9:27, "But I discipline my body and make it my slave." I.e., he refuses to let sin continue its domination over him! And so must we.

IV. SIN DESTROYS OUR SPIRITUAL NATURES

I will mention again that we human beings are dual or two-fold creatures. We not only have physical bodies, but also have souls (also called spirits, hearts, and inner beings). And sin destroys not only our bodies, but also and especially our souls. In our spiritual natures, because of sin, we are deceived, depraved, and defenseless.

DECEIVED. A major aspect of our spiritual nature is the mind or intellect. This is something we are using constantly in our waking moments. We are constantly thinking, reasoning, remembering, believing, and making decisions (among other things). Because of this prominent role of our minds in our life and personhood, it is no wonder that Satan's most persistent attacks upon us are aimed at our minds. And the thing Satan most wants to accomplish is to get us to believe lies and falsehoods—not just about God and religious things, but about the world in general. Jesus says about Satan that "he is a liar and the father of lies" (John 8:44). He is constantly trying to *deceive* us—and much of the time he is hugely successful. Sinners are, almost by definition, *deceived* people.

Prior to Christ's first coming, the whole world was in darkness (Acts 26:18) since the devil was busy "deceiving the nations" (see Revelation 20:2). That effort has been presently curtailed on its national scale by Christ's Great Commission to "preach the gospel to all creation" (Mark 16:15). In the final days before the second coming of Christ, though, this deceiving work of Satan will (with God's permission) be put into high gear again. Satan will go forth to "deceive the nations" again (Revelation 20:8). His activity will be marked "with all power and signs and false wonders, and with all the deception of wickedness for those who perish, because they did not receive the love of the truth so as to be saved" (2 Thessalonians 2:9-10).

This is a primary way that sin destroys us human beings. Despite the truth that is all around us, as men and women under the influence of sin we willfully close our eyes to that truth because it would interfere with the sinful lifestyles we want to live! This is why sinners "suppress the truth in unrighteousness" (Romans 1:18). This is why Paul refers to Satan's lies as "the deception of wickedness" (2 Thessalonians 2:10). This is why he tells us that sinners will be lost because they "did not believe the truth, but took pleasure in wickedness" (2 Thessalonians 2:12). This is why the primary condition for salvation is *faith*, the first part of which is *assenting to the truth of the gospel!* Becoming a Christian includes escaping from deception.

Sin deceives, but God's Word is truth (John 17:17).

DEPRAVED. Sin's destruction of the soul of man is rightly called *depravity*. Sinners are depraved in their spiritual natures. We usually avoid this term because we associate it with Calvinism, but the Calvinist error is in adding the word "total" to the noun. Calvinists believes in *total* depravity, meaning that the whole person is so depraved that he or she no longer as the free-will ability to respond positively to the gospel. They say that sinners are totally unable to believe in Jesus. This is wrong; the sinner's depravity is not *total*, but there *is* depravity.

Depravity is to the soul what disease is to the body. Sin, in the form of sinful desires and sinful acts, takes root in the spiritual aspect of our nature. Our spiritual strength, in terms of being able to resist temptation and say "No!" to sin, gets weaker and weaker. The soul becomes empty of the characteristics known as virtues, such as love, kindness, meekness, and self-control; and it becomes marked by those characteristics known as vices, such as covetousness, lust, pride, and hatred.

The Apostle Paul refers to this sinfulness of the soul as a state of spiritual death, of being "dead in your trespasses and sins" (Ephesians 2:1; see 2:5 and Colossians 2:13). Calvinists take this to the extreme of *total* depravity, saying that the sinner is unable to *believe* the gospel until regenerated. Colossians 2:12 shows that this is a false extreme, though, since Paul here teaches that the sinner is regenerated (raised from the state of spiritual death) "through faith." To avoid this false interpretation of the death references, it is more practical to think of depravity in terms of spiritual disease, as in Jeremiah 17:9, "The heart is more deceitful than all else and is desperately sick."

In Isaiah 1:5-6, the prophet draws a picture of what the depraved soul would look like if we could see it as we see the body. If we could see the sinful soul thus, how would it appear? "The whole head is sick and the whole heart is faint. From the sole of the foot even to the head there is nothing sound in it, only bruises, welts and raw wounds, not pressed out or bandaged, nor softened with oil." This shows us that sin is not just an *action* one performs; it is a *condition* in which one exists. What an enemy sin is!

DEFENSELESS. One other way sin destroys our spiritual nature is that it leaves us *defenseless* against our personal enemies, Satan and his demonic spirits. Though Satan is bound in this church age in the sense that he is unable to deceive whole nations (Revelation 20:1-3), he still is able to "prowl around like a roaring lion" (1 Peter 5:8) and attack us as individuals, especially through his minions, the demons or evil spirits. Paul describes them as the rulers and powers and world forces of darkness, "the spiritual forces of wickedness in the heavenly places" (Ephesians 6:12).

We saw above that Satan's main weapon is the *deceit* with which he attacks our minds; but he and the other fallen angels also attack our wills through *temptation*, and stand ready to invade our bodies through *demonization* (also called demon possession). Some think the demons are not active in the world today, but this is one of Satan's dangerous lies. They are still real and are still active; and sinners are *defenseless* against them without the armor that God supplies to us as Christians (Ephesians 6:13ff.).

The earliest generations of Christians, in the first few centuries of the church, assumed that all pagans were demonized and under the control of demons. Thus when they were preparing converts for baptism into Christ, a regular part of this preparation was an exorcism service in which the convert renounced the devil and his demons, and was anointed with oil. I once asked a respected church leader if he believed anyone is demonized in our time; his reply surprised yet pleased me. He said, "I believe they all are." I don't know if I can go that far, but I do think we do not take the demonic threat seriously enough. We cannot take for granted that just because we are Christians, we don't have to worry about such possibilities. After all, when Paul said, "Therefore, take up the full armor of God, so that you will be able to resist in the evil day" (Ephesians 6:13), he was giving a command to *Christians*! Without that armor, we are all defenseless against these enemies.

CONCLUSION

In this lesson I have tried to show how awful sin is by outlining the ways in which sin destroys us as human beings. It destroys our relationship with God and with the world in which we live. It also destroys our very nature, in both our body and our spirit. I don't want to end, though, without giving at least a summary of how any sinner can be delivered from this destructive enemy, sin. I usually speak of salvation as God's "double cure" of grace, using the phrase from the old hymn, "Rock of Ages." As I like to point out, if there is a double cure, there must be a "double trouble" (or "double curse") from which we are being delivered.

I'm not sure whether we do justice, though, to God's salvation by calling it just a "double" cure. Maybe it's a "triple" or "quadruple" cure—and maybe even more, if I could think up a word that represents *twelve* ways that God saves us from sin's destruction! The point is simply this: "Greater is He who is in you than he who is in the world" (1 John 4:4). God is greater than sin in every respect. As someone has said, sin is the destroyer, but God is the Restorer!

- Sin makes us desolate and separated from God, but God restores us to fellowship with Himself.

- Sin makes us detested by God, but through the blood of the Son we are reconciled to God.

- Sin makes us damned to hell, but Jesus takes our punishment on himself and brings us forgiveness and freedom from condemnation.

- Sin sinks our physical universe into the depths of disruption, decay, and distortion, but through the power of Jesus's resurrection this whole universe will one day be replaced by a new heavens and a new earth, in which dwells, not sin, but righteousness.

- Sin makes our bodies diseased and dead and dominated by sin, but God through Jesus Christ will raise us up into new, glorified, eternal bodies at Christ's second coming.

- Sin subjects our spirits to deception, but God's revealed and inspired Word shows us the truth.

- Sin infects our spirits with spiritual disease and death, but in our baptism God raises us up with Christ and sets us on the road to final and complete spiritual health.

- Sin strips us of our defenses against our enemies, but Jesus defeated those enemies in his work of death and resurrection and shares that victory with us.

And here is our battle cry: DEATH TO THE DESTROYER, AND ALL HAIL TO THE VICTOR!

THE AWFULNESS OF SIN

PART THREE: SIN DESPISES THE LAW

INTRODUCTION

"Sin is lawlessness." — 1 John 3:4

If you mention the word "law" to most people, they will probably think of criminal law, or civil law, or the laws of the land, or "law and order," or maybe a scofflaw. But if you say, "No, I'm talking about law as in the *Bible*," the first thing that will probably come to mind is the Law of Moses.

But here, when I say "law," I am referring to something more fundamental than either of these kinds of law. I am thinking mainly of *God's moral law*—the fundamental laws and rules and regulations that apply to all human beings at all times and in all places. These are the basic rules of right and wrong. They are the laws that govern every person's relationship with God and with one another. The moral law is the laws that apply to us *just because* we are human beings created by God. This is the universal law code given by the Creator to his human creatures.

There are other laws that God gives to specific people and specific groups of people, in specific times and for specific purposes. For example, God had special law commands for Noah and for Abraham; and He had a whopper of a special law code for the Israelite nation, i.e., the Law of Moses. There are some law commands in the New Testament that have been given just for those who are living now in the New Covenant era. For some reason, laws that fit into this category are called "positive" laws, as distinct from the moral law.

The Biblical writings include both positive (limited) laws, and the universal moral law. In the New Testament, even though some laws are new and apply only in this church age (e.g., instructions about the Lord's Supper), most of its ethical teaching is just the universal moral law being given in written form.

The moral law of God is as fundamental a part of the universe as are the laws of physics (or natural laws). They are just as necessary as the laws of physics for an orderly universe. *This is why sin is so AWFUL!* Sin is *lawlessness*. The very essence of sin is to *despise* the law of God. In this sense, every sinner is a true *scofflaw*. Sin is an attack upon the very fabric of the universe, upon its *moral* law and order.

Here we will explain why sin is so awful, because it despises the law of God.

I.   GOD AND LAW

God is the SOURCE of the law. The Bible describes God as a Lawgiver. Isaiah 33:22 says, "For the LORD is our judge, the LORD is our lawgiver, the LORD is our king." James 4:12 repeats some of this: "There is only one Lawgiver and Judge"—God Himself.

God is the PATTERN for the law. The law mirrors God's own holy nature and will. This answers the question, how does God decide what commandments to bind upon us, His creatures? Remember: He made us in His own image (Genesis 1:26-28), thus He wants us to be like him. "But like the Holy One who called you, be holy yourselves also in all your behavior; because it is written, 'You shall be holy, for I am holy'" (1 Peter 1:15-16). Here Peter quotes Leviticus 11:44-45.

This is true specifically for what we have called the *moral* law in the introduction above. This moral law is written on the heart of every human being (Romans 2:14-15), as part of what it means to be made in God's image. The Old Testament contains many of the law commands that are part of the moral law, but the Law of Moses specifically includes many instructions intended only for Israel under the Old Covenant. The latter would include laws governing temple worship procedures, as well as laws governing the details of Israel's social life. These positive laws are reflections of God's moral character only in a very general sense. The same would apply to the few positive laws in the New Covenant Scriptures.

The point is that most of God's laws ultimately represent this one thing: His own holy character or nature. All of His laws are expressions of His holy will.

God has a PURPOSE for the law, and that purpose is determined by His love for us. In fact, everything about the creation of this universe is related to His love. The two main purposes of creation are these: God created for the purposes of displaying His glory and sharing His goodness. We are thinking here especially about the latter. God made us human beings in His own image so that He could have a *love*-relationship with us, and share His goodness with us. And this is *why* He wants us to be holy as He is holy: because He loves us He wants us to be happy, and He knows that lives lived in imitation of His own holy character will be the happiest.

But where are the guidelines for such a holy and happy life? How do we *know* what God's holy character is? Answer: THE LAW! This is what the law is all about. God's holy nature is verbalized for us in His law. God's commandments show us His own holiness. Thus the law of God shows us how to live according to His purpose for us. It is the manufacturer's instruction book on how to match our moral character with that of God Himself.

The GOODNESS of the law is now made clear. Because of all of the above, "the law is good" (Romans 7:16). "So then, the Law is holy, and the commandment is holy and righteous and good" (Romans 7:12). God made the law "great and glorious" (Isaiah 42:21). "His commandments are not burdensome" (1 John 5:3). The law is *for* us, not *against* us. God wants us to obey it not just because He's the *boss* (which He is), but also because He *loves* us.

II. SINNERS AND LAW

Here I will explain how *sinners* relate to the law, before dealing with how *Christians* relate to it. At this point we have to distinguish two different ways the New Testament (especially Paul) uses the concept of law. On the one hand, "law" refers to the list of commandments that constitute the category of law, in the sense of our *law code*. All of our previous discussion has been about law in this sense, and this will be our main point here. On the other hand, sometimes (especially in Paul) the term "law" is used to refer to the *law system*, which is our attempt to get right with God, or go to heaven, by how well we are obeying our law code. In this sense, the law system of salvation is the alternative to (and the opposite of) the *grace* system of salvation (see Romans 6:14-15).

A. Sinners and the LAW CODE

First we will take a look at how sinners relate to God's law in the sense of the law code or list of commands we are obligated to obey. Based on Biblical teaching, we must recognize that in the final analysis, sinners *despise the law*. They despise it and want to be totally free from its constraints.

We see this in the very definition of sin that is given in 1 John 3:4. The key word in this verse is *anomia*, which is translated most frequently in one of two ways. Many versions, including the KJV, say, "Sin is the transgression of the law," i.e., the breaking of a command of the law. It is true that every individual act of law-breaking is a sin. This is what makes it a sin; in some way a *sinful* act is one that goes against the law of God.

There is another connotation to the word *anomia*, however, as indicated in the many versions of the New Testament that translate it thus:

"Sin is lawlessness." I.e., sin is not just an action; it is an *attitude* toward God's law. The very essence of sin is the attitude of hatred, hostility, contempt, rebellion, or opposition toward the law. Sin *despises* the law.

Nothing is more characteristic of our culture than this spirit of lawlessness, which is actually the spirit of *autonomy* and a rejection of authority. The Greek word for law is *nomos*, and we see it in *anomia*, which is basically just the root word *nomos*, preceded by the negating alpha. Putting the alpha (the Greek letter "a") in front of a word in the Greek language is like putting "anti-" or "non-" at the beginning of a word in English. Also, our word "autonomy" comes from the Greek words *nomos* ("law") and *autos*, which means "the self, oneself." Thus autonomy is the decision to be one's own lawgiver: "I will make my own laws, thank you!" It is the refusal to accept the authority of any law or rule that comes from outside oneself.

This attitude of lawlessness and autonomy is pictured in Psalms 2:1-3, where "the kings of the earth" declare their freedom from the Great King's law: "Why are the nations in an uproar and the peoples devising a vain thing? The kings of the earth take their stand and the rulers take counsel together against the LORD and against His Anointed, saying, 'Let us tear their fetters apart and cast away their cords from us!'" Here, the "fetters" and "cords" represent the laws of the sovereign God, and the words of these "culture kings" (influential human leaders) express very clearly the basic attitude of sin: "We refuse to be bound by the 'laws' of God!"

Why does this matter? What is so *awful* about despising and attacking the law? For one thing, it leads to the destruction of human society. But even more seriously—and this cannot be over-emphasized: the sinner's attack on law is an attack on *God Himself!* Remember point #I above: God and His law cannot separated! See Romans 8:7, "The mind set on the flesh is hostile toward God; for it does not subject itself to the law of God." Hostility toward God and refusal to submit to law go together. This is why so many people are professed atheists: "If we can just get rid of God, then we won't be bound by law anymore!"

This spirit of lawlessness permeates most of our culture, which as we know is shaped to a large extent by Darwin's theory of evolution. Those who have studied the life of Charles Darwin know that part of his motivation for devising evolutionism was his desperate attempt to escape a universe *designed* by God. This comes out in his open opposition to the influential Christian writer William Paley (1743-1805), who is famous for his popularization of the teleological argument for God's existence (the predecessor to the modern "intelligent design" argument). A modern parallel to Darwin's *anomia* is modern science's desperate search for evidence of life on planets other than Earth.

A major figure in the "Death of God" movement in the 1960s was Thomas Altizer, who wrote *The Gospel of Christian Atheism* (Westminster 1966). He fantasizes that Jesus was actually God incarnate, who deliberately became a human being so that he could be put to death—and stay dead. And he did this for our sakes, so that we would no longer be bound by "the alien power of the moral imperative"—i.e., a law that comes from outside ourselves. Thus the only way we can imagine that we are under some "moral demand" (i.e., law) is to be "estranged from Christ"— the "Christ" of his imagination, of course.

So Altizer invites us to "make a wager," to "bet that the Christian God is dead," and thus that we are free from obligation, guilt, and condemnation—because there is no longer any law! He says, "No, we are not guilty, says the Christian who bets that God is dead. His very bet denies the alien authority of the imperative, and refuses all that guilt arising from a submission to repression. He bets that he is even now forgiven, that he has been delivered from all bondage to the law, and that guilt is finally a refusal of the gift of life and freedom in Christ. Needless to say, such a wager entails a risk …." (From his book, pp. 144-146.)

The point is that to despise the law is to despise God Himself; to rebel against law is to rebel against God. To commit even one sin against

God (see James 2:10-11) is an accusation against God, an insult and a challenge toward God. As Stephen Charnock says, we are showing contempt for the holiness of God when we rebel against the law. "We cast dirt upon the holiness of God when we blame the law of God, because it shackles us, and prohibits our desired pleasures; and hate the law of God, as they did the prophets, because they did not 'prophesy smooth things.'" Also, "We are contrary to the law when we wish it were not so exact, and therefore contrary to the holiness of God, which set the stamp of exactness and righteousness upon it." (From his *The Existence and Attributes of God*, Kregel 1958 reprint, p. 507.)

The modern writer R. C. Sproul (forget for the moment that he is a Calvinist) makes this point in an excellent way in his book, *The Holiness of God* (Tyndale House, 1985), pp. 151-152:

> Sin is cosmic treason. Sin is treason against a perfectly pure Sovereign. It is an act of supreme ingratitude toward One to whom we owe everything, to the One who has given us life itself. Have you ever considered the deeper implications of the slightest sin, of the most minute peccadillo? What are we saying to our Creator when we disobey Him at the slightest point? We are saying **no** to the righteousness of God. We are saying, "God, Your law is not good. My judgment is better than Yours. Your authority does not apply to me. I am above and beyond Your jurisdiction. I have the right to do what I want to do, not what You command me to do"
>
> The slightest sin is an act of defiance against cosmic authority. It is a revolutionary act, a rebellious act where we are setting ourselves in opposition to the One to whom we owe everything. It is an insult to His holiness....

I will add one more selection from Charnock's work (p. 509): "It is no light thing, then, to fly in the face of God, to break his eternal law, to dash both the tables in pieces, to trample the transcript of God's own nature under our feet, to cherish that which is inconsistent with his honour, to lift up our heels against the glory of his nature, to join issue with the devil in stabbing his heart and depriving him of his life. Sin, in every part of it, is an opposition to the holiness of God."

B. Sinners and the LAW SYSTEM

As I explained at the beginning of section #II above, sometimes in the writings of Paul the word "law" does not refer specifically to any *law code*, but is referring rather to the *law system*, or the effort to gain eternal life by how well we are obeying our law code. Paul is referring to the law *system* when he says in Romans 6:14, "You are not under law but under grace." I.e., you are not under the law system as a way of getting to heaven; you are under the grace system.

Here we see a kind of paradox. Sometimes, when sinners who despise and abuse their *law code* DO begin to feel remorse and decide to change, the first thing they do is to abuse God's law in a different way! I.e., they try to use it in a way it was never intended to be used. By this I mean that they have accepted the idea that the only way for law-breakers to be right with the Lawgiver is to begin *obeying* His laws; and if we can obey it well enough from this point on, He will save us.

This is not the way salvation works, though. Once one has broken the law one time, and has thus become a sinner, there is no way anyone can ever get to heaven by how well he or she keeps the law from that point on. As Paul says, "By works of law—obedience to your law code—no human being will be justified in God's sight" (the meaning of Romans 3:20). Once we have sinned, the only way to be saved and to enter heaven is *by grace*, which is a wholly different way of relating to God. Rather than gain heaven by something *we* do, we are given the gift of heaven through our faith in something *someone else* has done: the death and resurrection of Jesus. "For we maintain that a sinner is justified by faith in Jesus, apart from a consideration of how well he is or is not obeying his law code" (the meaning of Romans 3:28).

By making salvation depend on faith rather than on law-keeping, are we nullifying the law or making it meaningless? Absolutely not! When we understand that we are saved by grace through faith, this upholds or establishes the law by allowing it to do what it is supposed to do in our lives (the meaning of Romans 3:31). And what it is supposed to do? It is supposed to show us how to be holy as God is holy! It is supposed to be the pattern after which we shape our lives!

The attempt to use God's law as a way of salvation (i.e., salvation by how well we obey the law's commands) seems to be a basic instinct in sinners. In my book on God the Redeemer, I spend a whole chapter (ch. 2, "Alternatives to Redemption") explaining how false religions and philosophies of the world understand salvation. One thing they all have in common is this: no matter what their concept of salvation entails, it is something that can be achieved only by the lost person's own efforts (i.e., by works). This is simply how sinners think. Thus when we present the gospel to them and attempt to lead them to salvation, we must be diligent in explaining to them that no one can be saved by the *law system* of salvation. (See my books on grace, e.g., *Set Free! What the Bible Says About Grace*, College Press, 2009; and *Saved by Grace*, Christian Restoration Association, 2018.)

III. CHRISTIANS AND LAW

How are Christians supposed to relate to the law of God? First and foremost, we must *reject* the *law system* as a way of being right with God. We must not try to use the law (law-keeping, commandment-keeping, living the Christian life, everyday obedience, being good, being holy) as a *way of salvation*. No one will ever be saved from hell by how well they obey their law code (Romans 3:20). This is because "all have sinned, and come short of the glory of God" (Romans 3:23). As a bridge back to God, the law falls short.

This is the whole point of Romans 1:18 – 3:20, namely, that salvation by the law system is impossible, because everyone has sinned. Paul shows how this applies to the Gentiles (those who have only general revelation) in Romans 1:18-32, and how it applies to the Jews (or to anyone who has

God's law via special revelation—including Christians) in Romans 2:1-3:8. Then he applies this truth to both groups together in Romans 3:9-20.

Then in the next section of Romans (3:21-5:21) Paul shows how God has provided a different way for sinners to be saved, and the only one that will really work. This sole effective system of salvation is GRACE, thus Romans 6:14 – "You are not under law but under grace."

The second thing we Christians must do in relating to the law of God is to *embrace* it in its form as a *law code!* We must *love* God's law, imitating David: "O how I love Your law! It is my meditation all the day" (Psalms 119:97). We must *obey* it and follow it as our way of life. It is a terrible error to assume, as some Christian leaders have done, that being saved by grace means we no longer have any law-commands that we have to obey! (For an example of this false view, see Carl Ketcherside, *The Death of the Custodian*, Standard 1976.) Against this virtual heresy, the Apostle Paul cries out "*Mē genoito!*" (Romans 6:1). "May it never be!"

What this means is that even though we are not under the law system, we are still under the law code that is included (mostly) in our New Covenant Scriptures. Even though we are under grace as our way of salvation, we still have a 100% obligation to obey every law commandment that applies to us in this New Covenant age. This is true because of *who God is* and *who we are* (see 1 Peter 1:15-16). Are we obligated, then, to obey God's commands? YES! It's the *law!*

If you love God, you will not only obey His law; you will *love* it! Loving God and obeying His law go together. This is how the Jews were commanded to regard their relation to God: "Now, Israel, what does the LORD your God require from you, but to fear the LORD your God, to walk in all His ways and love Him, and to serve the LORD your God with all your heart and with all your soul, and to keep the LORD'S commandments and His statutes which I am commanding you today for your good?" (Deuteronomy 10:12-13). Also, "I command you today to love the LORD your God, to walk in His ways and to keep His commandments and His statutes and His judgments, that you may live and multiply, and that the LORD your God may bless you in the land where you are entering to possess it" (Deuteronomy 30:16).

This is how Jesus explains it: "If you love Me, you will keep my commandments" (John 14:15). And John says, "For this is the love of God, that we keep His commandments; and His commandments are not burdensome" (1 John 5:3).

When we understand the relation between God and His law, we can see how it is really impossible to love God and not love His law at the same time. We will say with David, "And I shall lift up my hands to Your commandments, which I love" (Psalms 119:48). "O how love I Your law!" (Psalms 119:97). "Therefore I love your commandments above gold, yes, above fine gold" (Psalms 119:127).

The other side of this coin is this: if you love God, you will *hate sin*, because we know that God Himself hates sin. Here is another quote from Charnock's book (p. 509):

> He cannot look on sin without loathing it, he cannot look on sin but his heart riseth against it. It must needs be most odious to him, as that which is against the glory of his nature, and directly opposite to that which is the lustre and varnish of all his other perfections. It is the "abominable thing which his soul hates," Jeremiah xliv.4; the vilest terms imaginable are used to signify it. Do you understand the loathsomeness of a miry swine, or the nauseousness of the vomit of a dog? These are emblems of sin, 2 Peter ii.22. Can you endure the steams of putrefied carcasses from an open sepulcher? Romans iii.23. Is the smell of the stinking sweat or excrements of a body delightful? The word [filthiness] in James i.21 signifies as much. Or is the sight of a body overgrown with scabs and leprosy grateful to you? [See Isaiah 1:5-6.] So vile, so odious is sin in the sight of God.

When you love God, the very thought of sin will fill you with disgust and hatred. The very thought of your own personal sin will fill you with grief and repentance. Indeed, this is the very essence of repentance: hatred and grief toward one's personal sins.

CONCLUSION

There is only one bridge that can span the gap that sin has caused, and can take the sinner back to God; and that bridge is the gracious cross of Jesus Christ. But the law of God is the *guardrails* on the sides of that bridge, protecting us from false steps into the maelstroms and quicksand and snakepits of sin, indeed, into hell itself. Do not despise the law of God! Love it, embrace it, and obey it with all your heart.

The following hymn is Psalms 19:7-13 put into verse form by James McGranahan, and Psalms 119:97 intact:

The statutes of the Lord are right, and do rejoice the heart;
  The Lord's command is pure, and doth light to the eyes impart.
Unspotted is the fear of God, and ever doth endure;
  The judgments of the Lord are truth, and righteousness most pure.
They more than gold, yea, much fine gold, to be desired are;
  Than honey from the honeycomb that droppeth—sweeter far.
Moreover, they Thy servant warn how he his life should frame;
  A great reward provided is for them that keep the same.
O do not suffer sin to have dominion over me;
  I shall be righteous, then, and from the great transgression free.
O how love I Thy law, O how love I Thy law!
  It is my meditation all the day.
O how love I Thy law, O how love I Thy law;
  It is my meditation all the day.

THE AWFULNESS OF SIN

PART FOUR: SIN DEMANDS THE CROSS

INTRODUCTION

We are discussing the awfulness of sin. We have seen that sin is awful because it devastates God, destroys man, and despises the law of God. Now we will add one more thing to this list: sin is awful because it *demands the cross.*

Sometimes the question arises as to the necessity of the cross. When we think about the terrible agony involved in the whole crucifixion event, we have to ask, was the cross really necessary? Whatever God was trying to accomplish through the cross, could He not have achieved it some other way? This issue is brought up quite often by those who are critical of traditional, orthodox Christian belief. There was a time when liberal "Christians" attacked the cross as something that made Christianity a "slaughterhouse religion." In more recent times the critics are saying that the idea of the substitutionary atonement is a form of child abuse. Some have suggested that Christians should abandon the cross as a symbol of their faith and find a new symbol, maybe an egg.

The *AFA Journal* [from the American Family Association] for June 1997 (p. 19) had a report concerning an international conference held by the United Methodist Church, a denomination well known for its liberal leanings. The article, titled "Church Gathering Features Radical Speakers," was written by Mark Tooley. He reports that "one speaker declared that the crucifixion of Jesus Christ revealed an abusive Heavenly Father who is not fit for Christian worship. Instead, she urged that the church revere the baby Jesus along with all the world's children as equally little messiahs."

Tooley cites a speaker named Nancy Pereira as "explicitly rejecting the atonement of Jesus Christ." Lumping the cross together with Abraham's knife and Solomon's sword, she said that all of these "traditions" from the Bible portray a God who welcomes "child sacrifice." Here is a direct quote from her: "We have to find other expressions of salvation and liberation. We have developed a Christology with a tradition of the cross. That is a sacrificial Christology. It's a mechanism of salvation that heeds guilt, pain, whipping, and death. We have to look at Jesus' cross as a tragedy, a human episode without any sense of meaning."

Why is it that even "Christian" theologians such as Pereira see no "sense of meaning" in the cross? One reason, I suggest, is that they no longer have a valid understanding of the seriousness of sin. The weaker your view of sin, the weaker will be your view of the cross. Indeed, you ultimately can get to the point where the cross no longer makes any sense.

Here I will try to explain why sin is so awful that it demands the cross in the sense of Jesus the Son of God taking the place of sinners and suffering their deserved punishment in hell, so that the sinned-against God can forgive their debt of punishment and accept them back into eternal fellowship with Himself. I am thinking of how sin has brought about a separation between God and sinners, a separation that is such a wide and vast chasm that it would seem that nothing could bridge that gap of separation. It is into a scenario like this that the Christ of the cross comes, and performs an act of redemption which alone can provide a bridge across that vast sin-chasm. Jesus and His cross are the only bridge that can lead sinners back to God.

I. GOD'S DILEMMA

The first thing to establish is that God is faced with what looks like an unresolvable dilemma. What is a dilemma? One dictionary says it is "a situation requiring a choice between equally undesirable alternatives." That may sometimes be the case, but at other times there may be a situation where there are equally *desirable* alternatives, but only one of them can be chosen. And sometimes it just depends on how you are looking at it. A homeowner's dilemma may be to decide which bill to leave unpaid (or to pay)—electricity or rent?—because of shortage of funds. Or a parent's dilemma may be whether to attend (or to skip) Sally's piano recital or Billy's soccer game, since both were scheduled for the exact same time. Or maybe those Europeans who were hiding Jews from the Nazis during WWII had the dilemma of deciding which commandment to break (or which one to keep)—the sixth or the eighth.

God's dilemma is that He is faced with having to make a choice between two options, both of which are absolutely necessary. It would seem that the two options are exclusive, i.e., if He makes one choice , He cannot make the other—but He must do both! We may ask, how in the world did God get Himself into a situation like this? It begins with our understanding of the *nature* of God. First of all, one of the most basic attributes of God is that He is *righteous*. The essence of God's righteousness is that He absolutely must be true to Himself and true to all His attributes. He cannot act in such a way that His actions would contradict or violate His nature. E.g., since His nature is *truth*, He cannot lie or deceive.

How does this relate to the dilemma regarding the cross? The dilemma arises when we realize that there are two distinct and somewhat different sides to God's moral nature. Romans 11:22 sums up these two sides when it says, "Behold then the **kindness** and **severity** of God." Interpreting these in the light of other Scripture, we can say that the two sides of His nature are *love* and *holiness*. We know that "God is love" (1 John 4:8). And we also know that God says, "I am holy" (1 Peter 1:16).

His holy side includes his wrath, stated thus in Hebrews 12:29: "Our God is a consuming fire."

In what sense does this two-fold nature of God give rise to a dilemma? The problem arises when *human sin* appears on the scene. When God was making His decision to create this visible universe in which we live, He decided to populate it with personal beings made in His own image, who would have the gift of free will to enable them to freely choose to love, worship, and serve Him as their Creator. God made this choice, fully knowing that these human creatures would be able to use their free will to sin against Him; but for Him, the ability of these creatures to choose to *love* Him was worth the risk that they might choose to sin.

We know what happened next: mankind, in the persons of Adam and Eve, sinned against God and initiated a world population of sinners. It is this presence of sin in God's world that creates the dilemma for Him. The dilemma has to do with *how God is going to respond to sin*. What is the dilemma? It arises out of the fact that God is by nature both love and holiness, and His righteousness requires that each side of His nature *must* respond to sin in a way that seems to contradict or rule out the other.

On the one side, God's *holy* nature *demands* that sin must be punished, and that His wrath *must* be poured out upon every sinner. "Our God is a consuming fire"—that is His nature. And remember: God's righteousness requires that He be true to Himself and to His nature. But at the same time, God's *loving* nature *requires* nothing less than a sincere attempt to save sinners. "God is love"—*that* is His nature. And His righteousness requires that He be true to Himself and to His nature. How can God do both at the same time?

This creates what I call an unbelievable, unbearable *tension* within the nature of God. How can God be true to both sides of His nature at once? How can He satisfy the demands of His holy wrath, and the requirements of His holy love, at the same time? How can He both condemn and save sinners? I picture this tension within God as a huge rubber band that is being pulled in opposite directions at the same time. His love pulls Him in one direction, and His holy wrath pulls Him in the other direction. These are equally ultimate attributes of God; neither can cancel out the other. In the words of Romans 3:26, how can the righteous God be both *just* and *justifier*? ("Just" is the same word as "righteous.") So the question is, how can God justify (forgive the debt of eternal punishment) and at the same time be true to His nature as the Holy One?

II. THE CROSS RESOLVES GOD'S DILEMMA

For us human beings, we might ponder and agonize for a long time over a dilemma like this one. But let us not think that something like this was necessary for God. To Him it was not a dilemma in the sense that He (actually the three persons of the Trinity) had to sit around for a few million years while deliberating and brainstorming as to how to resolve the dilemma. No. Even before He made His decision to create the human race with the gift of free will, He knew that sin would be possible and that this dilemma would arise.

So from the very beginning, God had already resolved this dilemma in His mind. Even before the creation occurred, God had worked out HOW He would be able to save sinners and punish sin at the same time: THE CROSS! God Himself (God the Son) would become incarnate and go to the cross as a substitutionary sacrifice for mankind, suffering the equivalent of the eternal punishment for all of them. This was the "contingency plan" to be implemented if sin should happen. And since God in His foreknowledge knew that sin *would* happen, He foreknew also that the cross would be necessary and would happen. Speaking of Jesus, Peter says, "For He was foreknown before the foundation of the world" (1 Peter 1:20). Thus the man Jesus was "delivered over by the predetermined plan and foreknowledge of God" and "nailed to the cross by the hands of godless men" (Acts 2:23). Thus Jesus is "the Lamb who was slain from the creation of the world" (NIV).

Let us be clear. God did not *have* to create a world with free-will beings who would be able to sin; that was His free and sovereign choice.

But once He had determined to create the human race with free will, He was committed to the *possibility* of the cross; and once He foreknew that Adam and Eve would actually sin, the cross became a *necessity*. From this point on it was not optional. By this time, as the result of his own free, thought-out choice, God had no choice. WHY is it necessary? WHY does God no longer have a choice? Because the cross is the *only* way to resolve the dilemma created by sin! SIN DEMANDS THE CROSS. Nothing displays the awfulness of sin more than the cross.

Now we will explain *how* the cross resolves God's dilemma. In a word, the kind of death Jesus died on the cross *satisfied both sides of God's nature*, fulfilling the requirements of both His holiness and His love, enabling Him to be both just and justifier, at least of those who believe in Jesus (Romans 3:26).

First, in His experience of death in relation to the cross, Jesus satisfied God's HOLY nature by taking *upon Himself* the fullness of God's wrath due to the sins of the world. This substitutionary atonement is specifically taught in 2 Corinthians 5:21, which says that Jesus and sinners have essentially traded places: God "made Him who knew no sin to be sin on our behalf, so that we might become the righteousness of God in Him." He took our sin so that we can receive His righteousness. This means He took the *punishment* for our sin upon Himself. This reality is at the heart of the New Testament's description of Jesus as a "propitiation." "He Himself is the propitiation for our sins; and not for ours only, but also for those of the whole world" (1 John 2:2). The definition of propitiation is "an offering that turns away wrath." Jesus turned God's wrath away from us by taking that wrath upon Himself.

It is important to recognize that the suffering which Jesus endured as our propitiation was not just the physical pain derived from the human cruelty associated with crucifixion. Even as a human being, Jesus suffered untold emotional, mental, and spiritual agony, beginning as early as Gethsemane. But even this was not enough suffering to pay the price required to redeem the whole world. The deserved suffering planned for sinners is eternal suffering of some kind in what is known as hell. No mere finite human being could be a "stand-in" for this kind of requirement. That is why the propitiation had to be *infinite*—and the only infinite Being is God. This is why God the Son became a human being, so that He could suffer in our place not just as a man, but also and mostly *as God*. We cannot even begin to imagine the infinite suffering Jesus Christ was experiencing on the cross—a suffering that came upon Him not from human hands but from the very Holy Hand of God the Father. It was the equivalent of eternity in hell for the whole human race.

What Jesus was doing on the cross definitely puts the awfulness of sin into its proper perspective.

But wait—why was the cross *really* necessary? Why didn't God just consign the whole human race—all sinners—to hell and let them (us!) suffer their own punishment? Well, let's not forget the other side of God's nature: His LOVE. Jesus went to the cross not just to satisfy the wrath of God, but also to satisfy the *loving* side of His nature as well. It was not really the wrath of God that motivated Him (in the person of God the Son) to become the propitiation for our sins. It was actually His love: "In this is love, not that we loved God, but that He loved us and sent His Son to be the propitiation for our sins" (1 John 4:10). Yes, He could just send everyone to hell, and His wrath would be satisfied. But His *love* would not be satisfied! This is why the cross is necessary! This allows God to make salvation available to all of us without being untrue to the holy side of His nature. Thus Jesus did what He did to satisfy God's wrath *and* His love, but He actually did it FOR US – "on our behalf," says 2 Corinthians 5:21. Jesus gets the wrath, and we get the love. That's the essence of grace.

Near the beginning above, I pictured the sinner's dilemma as being separated from God by a huge sin-chasm. Now I will modify that picture by asking you to think of that symbolic chasm as being the Lake of Fire, after the image of hell found in Revelation 20:14-15 and 21:8. We sinners have no way to cross that chasm; there is no man-made bridge that can span it. But there is such a bridge! Jesus is that bridge, especially as the result of what He did for us on the cross. But to become that bridge, Jesus had to walk through that Lake of Fire in its full expanse.

In 1 Timothy 1:15 we read that "Christ Jesus **came into** the world to save sinners." Then we think of the wonder of the incarnation—that God would become a man and actually enter into our world and live as a man among us. Wow! What a sacrifice! "Though He was rich, yet for your sake He became poor" (2 Corinthians 8:9). Yes, that was quite a come-down. But here's the deal. The hard part about the incarnation was not how God the Son would *enter* the world, but *how He would leave it*! He knew He would have to die, yes. But He also knew that this would be no ordinary death! It would involve the eternal penalty deserved by all people because of their sin! It would involve bearing the infinite burden of the wrath of God while walking through the fires of hell! (The imagery here is figurative.)

Here is a kind of corny illustration, but think about it. You and your family are out exploring, and you come across the oddest thing: a sheer drop-off or cliff, dropping down about fifteen feet below into a pit. In this pit are all sorts of scary things: spiders, snakes, scorpions immediately below. And just beyond all this, blocking the only route out of the pit, is a hot spring feeding a great pool of boiling water. And just beyond that is a simmering volcano sending up flames and fumes.

All at once the youngest member of your family—a one-year old— toddles over the cliff and lands among the snakes and things in the pit below. You watch, horrified! He does not seem to be hurt, but you cannot reach him. How can you rescue the child? There is only one way. You have a small, light cord long enough to reach where the child is, but he is too young to grasp it and hold on to be pulled up. So you must jump off the cliff—a long jump, but you have no choice. You *must* jump. Then you can tie the cord around the baby and someone above, holding the other end of the cord, can pull him up; but the cord is too weak to pull you up. So— you must go down there. But once you do, there is no way for you to climb up the sheer cliff as a way out. The ONLY WAY OUT will be to walk across acres and acres of snakes, scorpions, and spiders, wade through a stretch of boiling water, and then cross a great field of burning tar and hot coals. And you *know* all of this before you jump in. But you *must* jump to save the child. Would you jump?

You see, here is the real wonder of Jesus's coming into the world—not just that "He came **into** the world," but that *He came anyway*, knowing what He would have to go through to **leave** this world! And the latter was a lot worse than snakes and boiling water and some hot coals.

Why was all this necessary? Because of the awfulness of sin! It was the only way that the holy and loving God could save us sinners from the very thing that Jesus went through so that we would not have to.

III. CROSSING THE BRIDGE

Sinners are separated from God by their sin. As we are symbolizing it here, lying between the sinner and God is the Lake of Fire. But Jesus came to build a bridge that would cross that chasm, and allow the sinner to be restored to fellowship with God. That bridge is the cross, representing the fact that Jesus has put Himself in our place and has suffered the equivalent of eternity in the fires of hell instead of us. But the sinner must willingly choose whether or not he wants to cross that bridge, leaving his sinful life behind and running into the arms of the Heavenly Father, like a prodigal son returning home. Thank God for the bridge, and thank God that many have crossed it!

When is this bridge crossed? When does the sinner experience this event of crossing the bridge? Can we Christians say that we have already crossed the bridge of the cross?

One major religion depicts the final judgment as involving this final test: walking across a very dangerous bridge. This is the Muslim religion, and it is their doctrine of Al-Sirat. They say that on the final day of judgment, every person will have to cross this bridge to get to the heavenly home. The bridge is as narrow as a hair, and is sharper than a sword. Beneath the bridge lie the fires of hell; if you fall off the bridge, you fall into hell forever. Your chances of making it across depend on how good your life on earth was, as judged by Muslim standards. It seems that Muslims take this horrible picture literally (rather than symbolically, as my picture of the bridge is meant to be).

We reject this concept found in the Al-Sirat doctrine, of course. There is nothing at all like it in the Bible. The fact is that you will already know your final fate before the Judgment Day actually comes. There is no bridge-crossing test you will have to pass at that time.

Another possible way of looking at the symbolic crossing of "the bridge of the cross" is that it is a way of viewing the entire Christian life. One gets on the bridge at conversion, then spends the rest of his or her life walking across the bridge and trying not to fall off. Thus we do not really know whether we will make our goal or not.

This is not the picture I am trying to conjure up in your minds when talking about the cross as the bridge that brings us back to God. I did make the comment in an earlier lesson that the law of God is like the guardrails of a bridge that are put there to keep us from falling off the path of righteousness, but this was a different and very limited illustration. It should not be equated with the idea of the Cross of Christ as a bridge to God. In fact the Cross-Bridge does not take a lifetime to pass over.

So when does the sinner cross over the bridge of the cross and return to God? The answer is simple: in the moment of conversion, when you pass from the unsaved state to the state of being saved (justified, initially sanctified, regenerated). Specifically, it happens in the moment of your baptism. And in my mind, I do not see us walking or running or crawling across that Cross-Bridge. I see Jesus carrying us across it.

Conversion is the time when we are restored to a right relationship with God, and it happens through the power of the cross, the power of Jesus's blood. The whole conversion experience is focused on the cross. This begins with faith itself, the very heart of which is "faith in His blood"—which is the correct translation of Romans 3:25, though few Bible versions besides the KJV get it right. (The Greek text says that Jesus is our propitiation *dia pisteōs en tē autou haimati*, literally, "through faith in His blood.") Also, repentance includes a hatred of the *sin* that nailed Him to the cross. Our confession includes confessing Jesus as the Christ, the "anointed one," the one who was anointed to be our Great High Priest to offer Himself as the sacrifice for our sins. And finally, the act of baptism is being buried into the very death of Jesus (Romans 6:1-4), where we come into contact with the justifying blood that He shed on the cross.

The point is this, that the moment you are raised up out of the waters of baptism, you have crossed the bridge of the cross! As a Christian that aspect of our journey home has been completed.

The practical result of crossing the bridge: assurance of salvation! It is very important to know that the rest of our life on earth is not some kind of test that we can never know whether we have passed or not until we get to the Judgment Day. No, we as sincere immersed believers are already "on the other side." We are in a saved, forgiven, born-again state. This is not because we have somehow magically progressed to a state of perfect obedience and 100% holiness; it is only because we are now under the blood of Jesus Christ. Our imperfect lives are in a sense hidden from God's eyes by the covering of Jesus's blood (see Isaiah 61:10; Romans 4:6-8).

This assurance of being saved should not be confused with the false doctrine of "once saved, always saved." We still have free will, and we can choose to stop believing just the same as we chose to start believing. But we have no plans to stop believing in Jesus! And here is the point: the only way you can become lost again is to give up your faith in Jesus. However, this does not give us a free ticket to sin all we want (see Romans 6:1ff.), since we still have a law code to obey, and since our believing and repentant hearts will be trying our best to obey that law. But it does mean that our individual sins do not separate us from God, unless they get so bad that they smother the life out of our faith (Matthew 13:22).

So let us rejoice in the power of the cross of Jesus Christ! This is where Jesus traded places with us. He took our sin, and he gives us his righteousness (2 Corinthians 5:21). Sometimes I get the impression from this verse that Jesus not only traded *places* with us, but traded *faces* with us. I.e., when God the Father was looking at Jesus on the cross, He saw *our* faces—the faces of sinners—and poured out His wrath upon that Lamb. What that means for us, though, is this: when God looks at us now—the ones who have crossed that bridge of His cross—He does not see the faces of sinners, but rather the sinless face of Jesus Christ. No wonder Paul can say in Romans 8:1, "Therefore there is now **no condemnation** to those who are in Christ Jesus"!

CONCLUSION

So where does that leave us now? When I was a child we used to sing a chorus, "Gone, gone, gone, gone! Yes, my sins are gone! Now my soul is free and in my heart's a song! Buried in the deepest sea—yes, that's good enough for me! I shall live eternally: praise God, my sins are gone!" I loved that chorus, and I still like—*most* of it. There is one serious theological problem therein, however. The fact is that our sins are NOT GONE! We still have a rather disturbing measure of *anomia*—lawlessness—in our lives. We commit sins, and our hearts are not completely pure from sinfulness.

It may not be as easy to sing or appreciate, but I would be happy if the song went like this: "Gone, gone, gone, gone! Yes, my GUILT is gone! … Praise God, my GUILT is gone!" That would be consistent with Romans 8:1, since "no condemnation" is the result of "no guilt." And it is the guilt and the punishment that are taken away in that conversion experience. In the moment of baptism, through faith in Jesus's blood, we become 100% justified by our faith in His blood; and as long as this faith survives, we will continue to be 100% justified (i.e., forgiven). And the basic meaning of justification is this, that the Judge looks at us and says, "No penalty for you!"

So back to the question: where does that leave us now? It leaves us with the task of pursuing our *sanctification*, which means that it is now our responsibility to actually *get rid of those sins* that are covered by the blood of Jesus. The guilt and condemnation are gone; now we must focus on the sin itself. This is why we have the gift of the Holy Spirit within us—to give us extra power to obey the commands of God's law, to give us the strength to be holy as God is holy. This is how you "work out your salvation with fear and trembling; for it is God who is at work in you, both to will and to work for His good pleasure" (Philippians 2:12-13).

We are not doing this in order to save ourselves, or to keep ourselves saved. We are doing it because we LOVE the God who created us, the loving God who gave us laws to show us how to live, the God who loved us even though we sinned, and the God who sent Jesus to take away the awful consequence of our sin by taking it upon Himself. How can we NOT love Him, and want to please Him? What greater motivation do we need than the CROSS?

THE AGE OF ACCOUNTABILITY: WHAT IS IT?

Notice that in the title of this essay, I do not say, "WHEN is it?" There is no set age when every child becomes accountable to God for the sins he or she has committed. Jewish law does set a specific time when children become accountable for their actions. For boys, that age is 13; for girls it is 12 or 13, depending on which branch of Judaism one is in. But this is not the Christian understanding of the "age of accountability." That point may be reached at different ages for different children, depending on their own individual circumstances.

So the issue is this: when trying to decide whether a specific boy or girl has reached that important turning point, what exactly are we looking for in the child? That is our question here.

We usually think of the age of accountability as the point of a young person's life when he or she becomes responsibly able to discern between good and evil. At this point of time the child becomes accountable or personally responsible for his or her sin. This is the time when one sees his or her own sin for what it really is: breaking the laws of God. It is also the time when one understands that he or she is facing serious eternal penalty from God for that sin.

Before this point in life, one is not accountable. I.e., the child has acquired no actual guilt and therefore is not liable for punishment. This does NOT mean, however, that before the child reaches that point, he or she does not know the difference between right and wrong, and has actually done nothing wrong, i.e., has not sinned. All would agree that even small children do things that are in themselves wrong, for example, tell lies. Also, the children are learning that some things are right and some things are wrong, and that the wrong actions will bring punishment. But in the beginning this system of rules and rule-breaking and punishment for rule-breaking is seen as a matter of one's relation to a parent or a teacher, and not one's relation to God. So the point is not that there is no knowledge of right and wrong, or no sin, or no guilt (even guilt feelings), or no punishment; rather, the point is that these sorts of things are not truly understood as *God*-related. I.e., the sin is against Mom and Dad, not against God; the punishment comes from Mom and Dad, not God.

This raises another point to consider. Often we have the idea that the child, upon entering the period of accountability, enters in complete innocence, which innocence remains his[1] state until he commits his first sin within this period of accountability. As a result he is no longer innocent, but now stands accountable for that first sin. The assumption is that upon entering the period of accountability, the child enters a probation period similar to that of Adam and Eve prior to the Fall, a time when he is morally pure and innocent. The innocence remains until the child consciously commits a sin in this probation period; from that time on, he is polluted.

I would here raise some questions about this construction of childhood innocence and the age of accountability. First, I affirm that the child, before entering the period of accountability, is not counted guilty before God of any sin, nor is he liable for any divine punishment. This is what the word means: he is not *accountable*. But second, and contrary to the common view, I also affirm that the child, while still in the pre-accountability stage, comes to know the difference between right and wrong, and will do many things that are wrong and sinful. I.e., he is not innocent and pure, like the pre-Fall Adam and Eve. He actually sins—but is not held accountable before God, because he does not understand *against whom* he has sinned. Thus he is not condemned the moment he does something wrong (except by a parent or teacher, perhaps). But that does not mean that the wrong things he does are not wrong—just that he is not accountable for them. Wrong things are *wrong* and always will be. The child entering the age of accountability does not do so with the option of extending some would-be, thus-far state of total innocence and moral purity—he has already been doing wrong things.

So I affirm that the transition from non-accountability to accountability is marked first of all by the realization of a difference between right and wrong *before God*, i.e., in relation to God and God's laws. He was already conscious of the difference between right and wrong, but was not aware of its transcendent consequences. But now there comes an awakening of conscience, a realization of responsibility *before God* for all the wrongs things he will do—and has already done.

The point is that we cannot ignore the things that were wrong that were done by the child before he became accountable for them to God. Once he becomes aware of the eternal consequences of the wrong things he has done, his conscience will be directed toward any of these that he can remember. What this means is that the child entering the age of accountability is not entering a period of *innocence*, but a period of *guilt*—guilt before God. This is the characteristic of this new period. This is the immediate result of his new knowledge. When the child realizes that his wrong deeds have been committed against a God who is now holding him accountable, he will now not only be counted guilty but will also have guilt *feelings*—even about wrong things already done. Even the child will be able to reflect upon his past wrongs and see, after reaching the age of accountability, that he is now guilty of these things before God his Lawgiver and Judge.

The important point here is that the child, upon entering the period of accountability, does not enter a period of innocence, but of guilt. He does not become consciously innocent (until committing his "first sin"), but he becomes consciously guilty before God. That is why it is called the "age of accountability" rather than the "age of sin."

One implication of this would be the cumulative effect (upon the child) of the degree of intensity of the wrongs he has done before becoming accountable to God. Compare, for example a child reared in a Godly home where he is taught to do good and to love God and Jesus, with one reared in a Godless environment, encouraged to do things that are wrong, and never taught to do something just because it is right. In this comparison, the former child will probably reach the age of accountability earlier than the latter, and probably with a deeper sense of guilt, even though probably with a lesser amount of wrongdoing. He will probably also have an earlier receptivity to the gospel. On the other hand, the latter child will probably reach the age of accountability later, and will probably have a lighter sense of guilt even though his intensity of wrong-doing will be greater.

In other words, the cumulative effect of any child's wrongdoing in the pre-accountability state will affect the way his sense of guilt develops as he approaches the state of accountability. Though the latter child may not feel his guilt as deeply as the former, his actual guilt will probably be substantially greater, and the intensity of the pollution or sinfulness of his nature will be greater and will probably hinder his ability and willingness to respond to the gospel. The practical application of this would be as follows: parents should not say to themselves, "Well, my child is too young to understand all this right-and-wrong stuff, so I will just let him do whatever he wants." No! The more firmly but lovingly the parents "train up the child in the way he should go" even in the young stages, the easier will be the transition into the age of accountability.

ENDNOTE

1 From this point on I will use male pronouns, with the understanding that what is being said applies to both male children and female children. And I do not feel guilty for doing so.

APPLAUDING AND ABETTING EVIL

The cover story of the May 2, 2013 issue of *Sports Illustrated* was about a pro basketball player named Jason Collins. After the 2012-2013 season was over, Collins announced that he is gay (i.e., homosexual). The reason it was deemed worthy to be a cover story in *SI* is that he was the first active male athlete from one of the four major North American professional team sports to publicly come out as gay. This made him (at least temporarily) famous; he became a darling of the media.

Many of those following the story noted the contrast between the way the media were treating Tim Tebow and the way they were treating Collins. One political cartoon had Tebow saying, "I'm a Christian," and the media guy responding, "Keep it to yourself." Then the cartoon portrayed Collins saying, "I'm gay," and the media guy gushing, "My hero!"

This whole tawdry episode has reminded me of what the Apostle Paul says about the pagan world in Romans 1:18-32. He declares that even those who have never had access to the Bible know, from what God has written on our hearts (Romans 2:15), that certain kinds of behavior are sinful. These include the list of sins he names in Romans 1:24-31, where he gives special attention to homosexualism (vv. 26-27).

In verse 26 the Apostle specifically condemns lesbianism: "For this reason God gave them over to degrading passions; for their women exchanged the natural function for that which is unnatural." This is the only specific reference to female homosexualism in the Bible, but it is clear enough. Then in verse 27 Paul turns to male homosexualism and declares it to be wrong in many ways: "And in the same way also the men abandoned the natural function of the woman and burned in their desire toward one another, men with men committing indecent acts and receiving in their own persons the due penalty of their error."

Then, after naming over a score of other sins, Paul affirms that we *all* know that these things—including homosexualism—are wrong: "They know the ordinance of God, that those who practice such things are worthy of death" (v. 32a). When Paul says, "*they* know," he means every human being: we all know that homosexual behavior is wrong because God has written it upon our hearts. Nevertheless, as the Apostle says in verse 18, it is characteristic of ungodly and unrighteous men to "suppress the truth in unrighteousness."

The widespread presence of all the sins mentioned in verses 26-31, especially homosexual behavior, indicates the depth to which our culture has sunk. But the Collins affair has turned the spotlight on another, even more demonic aspect of evil as mentioned by Paul in verse 32b, namely, that when someone is seen to be guilty of such sins, his fellow sinners "not only do the same, but also give hearty approval to those who practice them."

This "hearty approval" is what we have been witnessing ever since Collins made his announcement. This man has been not just defended but praised, congratulated, and indeed made into a hero for something that is the epitome of sin. Thus the guilt, the shame, and the condemnation fall not just upon the man himself, but also upon all who have spit into the face of God by glorifying and exalting this man and his sin.

In my *Commentary on Romans* (College Press, 1996), I said this about Romans 1:32: "Here Paul indicates that there is something worse than committing the sins named here.... Paul makes it clear that applauding and encouraging indulgence in sin is a serious aspect of the depravity of the Gentile world. The word means 'to be pleased along with, to consent with, to give approval to, to applaud.' Paul uses this very word to describe his participation in Stephen's death, though he did not throw any stones (Acts 22:20; see Acts 8:1). What makes this so evil is well described by Cranfield: 'Those who condone and applaud the vicious action of others are actually making a deliberate contribution to the setting up of a public opinion favourable to vice, and so to the corruption of an indefinite number of other people' (I:135). The best modern example of this is the plethora of movies, TV programs, books, musicians and entertainers in general who openly and brazenly promote all the forms of ungodliness and wickedness described here, and more" (I:168).

To the list in this last sentence we can add journalists, bloggers, sports writers, athletes, politicians, comedians, and talk show hosts, along with any others who "not only continue to do these very things but also approve of those who practice them" (v. 32b, NIV).

I have said elsewhere that there is a difference between having homosexual tendencies (i.e., "being" homosexual) and living a homosexual lifestyle (i.e., engaging in homosexual behavior). Regarding the former, it is possible for one to have same-sex inclinations, and at the same time recognize them as abnormal and try to suppress them and not engage in homosexual activity. I refer to this as the condition of homosexuality. Though this is not normal in terms of God's original, pre-curse creation, existing with the condition without acting on it is not sinful. On the other hand, engaging in homosexual activity (to which I refer as homosexualism) is indeed sinful, as Paul's teaching in Romans 1:26-27 makes very clear.

Now, I do not know for sure into which category Mr. Collins falls. If the former, I pray that God will give him strength to live with it without acting upon it. But I am assuming, based on the public announcement and the media uproar about it, that he is a practicing homosexual. I think it is safe to say that if he were simply confessing that he is a non-practicing homosexual, he would not be attracting all the praise and attention that is being heaped upon him by our pagan culture.

What I am saying here about this one incident and the one kind of sin equally applies to public glorification of *any other sin*. Our media, especially those representing the entertainment industry, celebrate all kinds of sexual immorality and other kinds of sins as well.

The lesson for us is this, that we all need to be conscientious regarding our attitudes toward sin. It is indeed important to avoid sins themselves. But how often do we find ourselves laughing at others who indulge in sins, or joking about sinful behavior—whether in real life or in fiction? How often do we catch ourselves being nonchalant and unconcerned about the ever-expanding cesspool of evil that threatens to inundate our world? To be holy as God is holy (1 Peter 1:15-16) includes hating sin with the same passion that God hates it.

SECTION FOUR

DEATH

YOUR WORST ENEMY: DEATH!

INTRODUCTION

We all know about villains: Darth Vader, Hannibal Lecter, Freddy Krueger, Godzilla, the Joker, the Penguin—to name a few fictitious ones. In real life we could name Stalin, Hitler, Idi Amin, Pol Pot, and Sadam Hussein. The worst villain of all, though, is DEATH!

The *event* of death may be defined simply and briefly as the loss of life. As a *state*, death is simply the absence of life (where life is the normal state). It is a state of separation from the source of life. We speak of a battery that has lost its life or power as being *dead*. An electrical wire that is connected to its source of power is a *live* wire.

In the Bible there are three kinds of death as it applies to human beings. One is *spiritual* death, which is the state of the unbelieving, unregenerate sinner whose soul is dead to God. This state is described in Ephesians 2:1, 5: "And you were dead in your trespasses and sins ... when we were dead in our transgressions." See Colossians 2:13 also. The second form of death is *physical* death, which happens in the moment when the soul or spirit leaves the body. As James 2:26 says, "The body without the spirit is dead." The last and most devastating kind of death is *eternal* death, in which both body and soul exist in a state of separation from God forever (Matthew 10:28). See Revelation 20:14: "This is the second death: the lake of fire." Revelation 21:8 says that sinners are condemned to "the lake that burns with fire and brimstone, which is the second death." See also 2 Thessalonians 1:9.

Why should we want to think about death? Because this is what our salvation is all about! Jesus came to save us from this enemy! He tells us in John 10:10, "I came that they may have life"! What follows here is, first, BAD NEWS; then, GOOD NEWS.

I. THE BAD NEWS: DEATH IS OUR ENEMY.

Why do we say this? Why should we think of death as our enemy? We say it for five reasons. First, death is our enemy because it is contrary to our NATURE. Human beings were created to *live forever*. Genesis 2:7-9 tells us that when God created the first man, Adam, he breathed into the man's nostrils "the breath of life; and man became a living being." Then he placed him in the Garden of Eden, in the midst of which was "the tree of life." This shows that, contrary to evolutionary theory, human beings were not intended to die. There is no such thing as dying from "natural causes." Human death is *unnatural*. Even *old age* is unnatural!

The second reason death is our enemy is because it is the result of SIN. The whole human race dies physically because of Adam and Eve's sin. In Genesis 2:17 God warned our first parents not to eat from another tree in the Garden of Eden, "the tree of the knowledge of good and evil." God said, "In the day that you eat from it you will surely die." And this death penalty referred not just to Adam. Romans 5:12 says, "Through one man sin entered into the world, and death through sin, and so death spread to all men, because all sinned"—in Adam. 1 Corinthians 15:22 sums it up: "In Adam all die."

Death comes not just from Adam's sin but also from personal sin. In Romans one and two, Paul affirms that all human beings are sinners. In chapter one, after naming a long list of sins, in verse 32 he declares that those who sin "know the ordinance of God, that those who practice such things are worthy of death." He then states in Romans 6:23, "The wages of sin is death." And in Romans 8:10: "The body is dead because of sin."

James 1:15 adds, "When sin is accomplished it brings forth death." 1 Corinthians 15:56 says, "The sting of death is sin."

The third reason death is our enemy is because it reigns as an alien KING who has usurped power over the whole earth. In Romans 5:14, 17, talking about the effect of Adam's sin, Paul uses the Greek verb *basileuō*, meaning "to reign as king." He says, "Death **reigned as king** from Adam to Moses, even" over little children. "By the transgression of the one, death **reigned as king** through the one." Here death is personified as a tyrant having everyone under its power. It controls how we approach life as such. Life becomes just the effort to avoid or delay death. Consider our preoccupation with health care and safety. In 2014, 28.5% of our U. S. federal budget was devoted to health care expenses.

Here is a fourth reason why death is our enemy: it a tool of SATAN. Hebrews 2:14-15 says, "Since the children share in flesh and blood, He Himself likewise also partook of the same, that through death He might render powerless him who had the power of death, that is, the devil, and might free those who through fear of death were subject to slavery all their lives." Satan and his evil demons devote most of their energy trying to lead us into sin, which as we know leads to the penalty of death. Thus we are slaves to the fear of death until it overtakes us, for the reason named in the next point.

Indeed, and finally, death is an enemy because it is the door to the FINAL JUDGMENT, as Hebrews 9:27 says: "It is appointed for men to die once, and after this comes judgment." This is a main reason why many live in fear of death—not only because of death itself, but because of what we know lies beyond it.

No wonder we hate death so much! No wonder we try to put it off as long as possible! No wonder, as we get closer and closer to it, we feel more and more haunted by fear and dread! Death is our enemy! BUT – this is not the end of the story. There's more – and it's *good* news!

II. THE GOOD NEWS: DEATH IS A *DEFEATED* ENEMY!

Death is not just OUR enemy; it is also GOD'S enemy! This is indeed good news! Though God Himself imposed the penalty of death upon us, this was not his deepest desire. From the beginning, God planned to personally confront this enemy and destroy it! This is why God became a man in the person of Jesus Christ! Jesus came as the *Superhero* to confront and conquer the villain that has laid waste to God's creation. This was the purpose of his death and resurrection. See Hebrews 2:14-15 again.

Here is the bottom line: Jesus has *defeated* the enemy, death! One word that sums up Jesus's work: *VICTORY!* Victory over all *his* enemies, and ours: sin, death, and the devil! All these villains were defeated by our Superhero, Jesus Christ! See 2 Timothy 1:10: God's purpose "has been revealed by the appearing of our Savior Christ Jesus, who abolished death and brought life and immortality to light through the gospel." My fantasy is that if Jesus lived among us today, the only shoes he would wear would be NIKE! That's because the Greek word for "victory" is *nikē* (pronounced *NEE-kay*.)

Here is the essence of the good news: because of Jesus, if you are a Christian, death has been, is being, and will be defeated in YOUR life. This is true of all three kinds of death. First, *spiritual* death has *already* been defeated in you. In your baptism you were raised from the dead: God, "when we were dead in our transgressions, made us alive together with Christ" (Ephesians 2:5). Colossians 2:12-13 says specifically, "Having been buried with Him in baptism, in which you were also raised up with Him through faith in the working of God…. He made you alive together with Him." You have thus "passed out of death into life" (1 John 3:14; see John 5:24).

Second, it is also true that *eternal* death – condemnation to hell, the lake of fire – has *already* been defeated *for* you – by Jesus! In your baptism you were forgiven; you were justified by the blood of Jesus (Acts 2:38; Romans 5:9). See especially Romans 8:1: "Therefore there is now no condemnation for those who are in Christ Jesus." To be justified means that the Judge is saying to you, "NO PENALTY FOR YOU! No condemnation for you! No hell for you!" As long as we continue to trust in the saving death of Jesus, the eternal death of the lake of fire is not in our future.

But what about the third form of death, *physical* death? We still have to die physically. Does that mean that death wins after all? No! Consider this: our Superhero, Jesus, died and was buried. Was that the end of *Him*? Did death win over Jesus after all? NO! Jesus died, but death does not have the last word! LIFE does!

On resurrection morning, Jesus our Superhero defeated the villain of death. He came out of his grave! He fought the enemy death, and He won! He delivered the death blow to death itself! In Revelation 1:17-18 He announces His victory: "Do not be afraid; I am the first and the last, and the living One; and I was dead, and behold, I am alive forevermore, and I have the keys of death and of Hades."

This victory over death will also be ours. When Jesus returns, there will be a resurrection of the dead. (See 1 Corinthians 15:25-26.) Our assured hope is well stated in 1 Corinthians 15:52-57 – "In a moment, in the twinkling of an eye, at the last trumpet: for the trumpet will sound, and the dead will be raised imperishable, and we will be changed. For this perishable must put on the imperishable, and this mortal must put on immortality. ... Then will come about the saying that is written, 'Death is swallowed up in victory. O death, where is your victory? O death, where is your sting?' ... But thanks be to God, who gives us the victory through our Lord Jesus Christ." As Revelation 21:4 promises, in the final heaven "He will wipe away every tear from their eyes, and there will no longer be any death."

In conclusion, how shall we face our coming death? Here is my counsel: feel free to HATE it. Feel free to face it with reluctance, sadness, and mourning. But DO NOT FEAR IT! Death is a DEFEATED enemy. Declare with David (Psalm 23:4): "Even though I walk through the valley of the shadow of death, I fear no evil, for You are with me." We are facing this enemy death with Jesus our Superhero at our side. BRING IT ON!

IN THE FACE OF DEATH[1]

DEATH! The fact of it or even the very thought of it can stir up the deepest feelings of which a human being is capable. Particularly the death of a loved one or of a friend moves us with deep emotions.

What are these feelings which are evoked by the experience of death? Reflection upon them now may enable us to cope with them when we are next forced to encounter this, our relentless enemy.

SORROW. The most obvious feeling elicited by encounter with death is sorrow or sadness. When one from our circle of friends or from our family dies, we are naturally filled with sorrow; for death forces upon us at best a period of separation from one whom we love. Such sorrow is not a matter of shame; nor is it something to be repented of. It is not something to be suppressed in the guise of manliness; for sorrow is a human emotion, and even the strongest of men are human. Neither need it be suppressed in the name of strong Christian faith; for such sorrow is not a threat or a contradiction to faith.

RAGE. Another feeling evoked by the event of death is that of anger or rage. Often one finds his anger either willingly or unwillingly being directed toward God. How many bereaved fathers have shaken their fists in God's face and blasphemously accused Him of the death of their children? How many grieving spouses have angrily blamed God for the loss of their mates?

Now, such rage itself is understandable. That God should be the object of it, however, is not. What should be the proper object of this anger? Death itself; and sin, which is the real cause and sting of death (1 Corinthians 15:56); and Satan, who holds the power of death (Hebrews 2:14).

The incarnate Christ Himself exhibited a divine rage against death.[2] When Jesus came upon the earth, He came as a human being with true human emotions. He developed close friendships with some of His disciples. John 11 tells how Jesus reacted in the face of the death of one of those close friends, Lazarus of Bethany.

When Lazarus became mortally ill, Jesus was notified; but He did not leave immediately for His friend's home. He delayed His arrival until four days after Lazarus's death and burial; and then He found Lazarus's sisters and friends weeping and engulfed in sorrow. When Jesus witnessed this sorrow, He, too, wept. But why? He was moved not just with sympathetic sorrow, but with rage. John 11:33 says, "When Jesus therefore saw her weeping, and the Jews who came with her also weeping, He was deeply moved in spirit and was troubled." The Greek word translated "deeply moved" is *embrimaomai*, which has the sense of snorting with anger and displeasure (according to my Arndt and Gingrich Greek Concordance). The American Standard Version footnote reads, He "was moved with indignation in the spirit."[3] The same expression is used in verse 38, "So Jesus, again being deeply moved within [being enraged within Himself, being moved with indignation in Himself], came to the tomb."

The emotion pulsing through the human heart of Jesus at this event of His friend's death was no less than rage against death itself. Jesus knew death for what it really is, the enemy of mankind. This is exactly why He came among men, "that through death He might render powerless him who had the power of death, that is, the devil, and might free those who through fear of death were subject to slavery all their lives" (Hebrews 2:14-15). The raising of Lazarus for a few more years of earthly life is a symbolic prelude to His own death and resurrection, by which He conquered forever this enemy.

That death should continue to arouse feelings of rage should not surprise us. Let us take care, however, to direct such feeling toward their proper object, death itself, and not toward the God who Himself is enraged at death and who has acted to overcome it.

DREAD. A third feeling elicited by the fact of death is that of fear and dread. The death of a friend or relative reminds us of the brevity of life and of the certainty of our own death.

But again, this is specifically why Christ came, and why He died and rose again. He knew and was touched by our fear of the enemy, death; and He knew how such fear can enslave us, and can permeate our whole life with the feeling of despair and hopelessness. Thus He came to conquer this enemy and to abolish this fear. See again Hebrews 2:14-15.

This is what Jesus Christ is all about; this is what Christianity is all about; this is what the church is all about. Jesus came to build a church against which the forces of death are powerless. He said during His earthly ministry that upon the solid rock of His own deity and Messiahship He would build His church, "and the gates of Hades will not overpower it" (Matthew 16:18). The "gates of Hades" rightly means "the forces of death." Some New Testament versions translate it as "the power [or powers] of death." He who trusts in Jesus Christ and belongs to His church need not fear death. To belong to Jesus Christ is to belong to the one who has conquered death. *His* victory becomes *our* victory. As He said to Martha at the occasion of the death of Lazarus, "I am the resurrection and the life; he who believes in Me will live even if he dies, and everyone who lives and believes in Me will never die. Do you believe this?"

So how must we feel in the face of death today? The answer is clear. Let there be sorrow indeed, and even rage, when a loved one dies, or when we ourselves are facing death. But for those who belong to Jesus Christ, the victor, let there be no fear, no despair at the prospect of death.

ENDNOTES

1 This item originally appeared in the *Christian Standard*, August 8, 1971, p. 9. It is being reprinted here by permission of Christian Standard Media.

2 See B. B. Warfield, "The Emotional Life of Our Lord," in *The Person and Work of Christ*, ed. Samuel G. Craig (Philadelphia: Presbyterian and Reformed, 1950), pp. 114ff.

3 Writing from the perspective of the twenty-first century, I can say that "The Message" translation and the New Living Translation both translate this word as "a deep anger welled up within him." The Holman Christian Standard Bible renders it, "He was angry in His spirit."

WHAT HAPPENS TO US WHEN WE DIE?

QUESTION: What happens to us when we die? Do believers go directly to heaven at the moment of death? What is the relation between our death, on the one hand; and Christ's second coming, the resurrection, and the final judgment, on the other hand?

ANSWER: The answers to these questions require a lot more space than is available here. I have discussed them fully in my College Press books, *The Faith Once for All* (see the final chapters) and *Bible Prophecy and End Times*. Here I can only summarize my approach to these issues.

First, a proper understanding of the afterlife requires that we accept the Bible's clear teaching that human beings are twofold in essence, i.e., each of us is composed of a physical body and a spiritual soul. When we die, the body and the soul become separated from one another; the body itself enters the state of death, while the soul experiences death but does not itself die. Our dead bodies are usually placed in some sort of grave, which the Old Testament calls Sheol and the New Testament calls Hades. The crucial issue is what happens to the soul.

Though some disagree, I am convinced that at death the soul (being separated from the body) continues to exist individually, consciously, without a body, and subject to the passing of time. It is thus in a state of waiting, i.e., waiting for the end of the *aion* (age) of this first (old) creation and for the second coming of Christ. When Christ returns the soul is joined once more to a body in the event called the resurrection of the dead.

The replacement bodies for the wicked (the lost) and for the righteous (the saved) will not be the same.

In the interim, or the intermediate state between our death and resurrection, the conscious souls of the wicked are banished to another place also called Hades (Luke 16:23), a term that specifically refers to the realm of the dead, the place where death reigns. The grave is called Hades because it is the receptacle for dead *bodies*, both of the lost and the saved. The temporary place inhabited by the souls of the deceased lost is also called Hades because these *souls* are *spiritually* dead.

The souls of the saved who die, however, do not go to Hades, because they are in a state of spiritual *life*, not spiritual death. Their temporary post-mortem home is called Paradise (Luke 23:43), where the Jews thought of themselves as being ensconced in Abraham's bosom (Luke 16:22) and Christians expect to bide their pre-judgment time in the presence of the Lord Jesus (2 Corinthians 5:6-8; Philippians 1:23).

Here are two things we need to know about this temporary place of waiting. First, the Paradise to which our souls are transported when we die is called "heaven," but it is not the *final* heaven, the "new heavens and new earth," the new universe in which we will live forever (Revelation 21 & 22). This final heaven does not even exist yet (see 2 Peter 3:8-13). Rather, the heaven to which we go at the moment of death is the *angelic* heaven, described by John in Revelation 4-5 (see Isaiah 6:1-7). This is part of the created invisible universe (Colossians 1:16), the natural home for all angelic creatures. God has established a majestic throne room in this angelic realm, and he presents himself there at all times to the angels in a permanent theophany (visible form). This throne room is the center of the Paradise to which our souls are transported at the moment of death.

The second thing we need to know about this temporary place of waiting is that this divine throne room in the angelic world is the *same destination* for both those Old Testament saints who died before Christ's death, resurrection, and ascension, and those Christian saints who die afterwards. Some think the souls of the Old Testament saints were not yet admitted to this "heaven," but had to wait in a sort of holding pen, called the *limbus patrem* ("limbo of the fathers") until Christ's death and resurrection. Only then, according to this view, could they actually enter this heavenly throne room, and they are thought of as accompanying Christ at his ascension and entrance into heaven. This is all fiction, however. The souls of Old Testament saints entered this heaven as soon as they died; they simply did not experience the presence of Christ in that place until his ascension and enthronement. (For these pre-Christian saints, existing in "Abraham's bosom" would have seemed to be the epitome of glory and bliss.)

Thus in this sense, the soul of every saved person has entered or will enter this angelic heaven at the moment of death, to await the end of this present era. Many have already been waiting there for a long time, and there we will wait in comfortable bliss until the time for the second coming of Jesus.

When the Father initiates the grand event we call Christ's second coming, Jesus will arise from his place on the throne and will pass through the dimensional barrier that separates the invisible realm of angels from the visible world we inhabit. He will take with him his holy angels as well as the souls of the saved who have been patiently waiting for this moment. This is the time when the dead receive their new bodies, and the living saints are transformed into a glorified body without having to experience death.

Then in our new bodies, we (the just and the unjust alike) are all taken back into the heavenly throne room for the event called the Final Judgment. While this is taking place, the old physical universe is being replaced by the new heavens and new earth. Once the Judgment Day has been completed, the wicked are consigned to hell in their souls as clothed in their ghastly replacement bodies, and the saved are transported in their souls as clothed in their new glorified bodies to their eternal dwelling place, the new earth surrounded by the new heavens (new universe). There we shall live "happily ever after" in the presence of the glorified Christ, and in the presence of a new theophany of God, parallel to the one he still maintains in the angelic throne room for the benefit of the angels. See Revelation 21 and 22.

HADES: WHAT IS IT?

QUESTION: I have seen the word "Hades" in the New Testament several times, but I am not sure what that means. Can you explain it?

ANSWER: I can try. First, the Old Testament equivalent to Hades is Sheol, which appears about 65 times in Old Testament writings. The Greek Old Testament (the Septuagint) translates this word with Hades almost every time. The New Testament then uses Hades ten times (or 11 if 1 Corinthians 15:55 is counted). The main thing to remember is that these words are always connected with DEATH. They are the place or location of the dead. For this connection see Psalms 18:5; Proverbs 5:5; Isaiah 28:15; Revelation 1:18; 6:8.

To properly understand these terms we must first of all accept the full inspiration of the whole Bible and thus the unity and consistency of the contents of its teaching. Second, we must accept the Bible's teaching that human beings consist of two parts, the physical body and the spirit or soul. These are meant to exist together but are separated at the point of physical death. Finally, we must accept the fact that there are three aspects of the death that has fallen upon the human race as the result of sin: the physical death of the body; the spiritual death of the soul (Ephesians 2:1, 5); and eternal death in hell, the lake of fire, which is "the second death" (Revelation 20:14; 21:8).

Much of the confusion about the nature of Hades (Sheol) is the result of the denial of the reality of the soul or spirit as a genuine and separate aspect of human nature. Such a denial is central in the theology of Jehovah's Witnesses and Seventh Day Adventists, for example. The soul's existence is also becoming more and more questioned even in evangelical circles. Those who thus see human beings as bodies only will never properly understand the nature of Hades. (On the dualistic nature of man, see my book, *The Faith Once for All*, pp. 134-147.)

How then shall we understand Hades, the place and power of death? First of all, we must see that at times Sheol in the Old Testament and Hades in the New Testament refer to the *grave*, which swallows up the *bodies* of those who die, righteous and wicked alike. Those who deny the existence of the soul often say that Sheol and Hades *always* refer to the grave, but they are wrong. Some (such as Robert Morey) say these words *never* refer to the grave, but this too is wrong.

On the one hand (contra Morey), in some texts Sheol/Hades clearly means the grave. In its sense of "the place of the dead," Sheol/Hades is the place beneath the surface of the earth where dead bodies are buried. As such, both the righteous and the wicked enter into Sheol/Hades, the enemy which captures and devours every member of Adam's race. In this way, even for the righteous, death seems to be the victor, since the grave swallows us all and turns our bodies back to dust (see Psalms 89:48; 116:3; 141:7; Isaiah 38:10). In this sense Sheol/Hades is something to be dreaded and feared, something from which we all long to be delivered and redeemed (Psalms 49:14-15; 86:13; Hosea 13:14). This is the light in which Psalms 16:10 must be understood: "For You will not abandon my soul to Sheol; nor will you allow Your Holy One to undergo decay." (Here the word "soul" has the sense of "person, self"; "my soul" means "me, myself.") In Acts 2:27, 31 Peter cites this as a prophecy of the resurrection of Jesus's body from the tomb, whereby "He was neither abandoned to Hades, nor did His flesh suffer decay." This refers only to Christ's body as buried in and raised from the grave (Sheol/Hades), not to the state or activity of His spirit between His death and resurrection.

On the other hand (contra those who deny the soul's existence), in some texts where Sheol/Hades refers to a specific location, it does *not* refer to the grave as the receptacle of the *body* but to the place to which the *spirits* of *some* of the dead are taken, where they will exist in their intermediate (bodiless, conscious) state until Christ's return. Since Sheol/Hades is the place of the *dead*, only the souls of the *wicked* are put into Sheol/Hades in the sense of the waiting place for disembodied souls (see Job 24:19; Psalms 9:17; 31:17; 55:15; Proverbs 9:18; 23:14; Isaiah 14:13-15; Matthew 11:23). The souls of the righteous do not enter Sheol/Hades, since their souls are not in a state of spiritual death but have been made alive through God's resurrection power (Ephesians 2:5-6; Colossians 2:12-13). Thus we should not think that Sheol/Hades is occupied by the souls of the righteous and the wicked alike (Psalms 49:14-15; 86:13; Proverbs 15:24).

As the place where the wicked abide until judgment, Sheol/Hades is seen as an enemy or captor in all its terror. In Jesus's story of the rich man and Lazarus, only the rich man (personifying the wicked in general) is said to be in torment "in Hades" (Luke 16:23).

In both of its specific meanings, (1) the grave as the receptacle of the bodies of all men, and (2) the intermediate dwelling place for wicked souls, Sheol/Hades is mankind's enemy, a foul force conquered by the redeeming work of the crucified and risen Christ (Revelation 1:18) and from which we find refuge in the church (Matthew 16:18). In the end it will be finally destroyed in the lake of fire (Revelation 20:14).

Where, then, do the souls of the righteous go when separated from the body at death? Their destiny is never called Sheol or Hades. They are described as being in Abraham's bosom (Luke 16:23), in Paradise (Luke 23:43), "at home with the Lord" (2 Corinthians 5:8), and under the heavenly altar (Revelation 6:9). We may refer to this simply as Paradise (see 2 Corinthians 12:4), which should not be considered as just one section of Hades. Righteous souls have been "made perfect" (Hebrews 12:23), and that includes being made fully alive in a spiritual sense. They no longer have the stench and penalty of spiritual death about them, and thus are not proper citizens of Hades, which is the place of *death*. The righteous are "in Hades" only in the sense that their *bodies* are in the grave.

Where are Paradise and Sheol/Hades located? Paradise, as the place where the souls of the righteous dead exist in their intermediate state, is equivalent to or at least adjacent to the heavenly throne room district of the invisible universe created for the angelic race. This conclusion is based on two facts. First, John saw the souls of at least some of the righteous dead under the altar of this heaven (Revelation 6:9). Second, when we die our souls will be in the presence of Christ (2 Corinthians 5:8; Philippians 1:23), and Christ himself in his glorified human existence is presently in this heavenly throne room (Acts 7:55; Revelation 3:21; 5:6, 13). When we die, our souls will awaken in conscious bliss in that blessed place.

But where is Sheol/Hades, the place into which the souls of the wicked are ushered at death? We can only speculate about this. But based on the above, I infer that this too is a part of the invisible universe, a distant or nether region far from the presence of God and the glorified Christ, perhaps adjacent to the place called Tartarus occupied by some fallen angels (2 Peter 2:4). It is a place of darkness (Job 17:13), gloom and suffering, without light and without hope. It is the place where lost human beings await the final judgment and their eternal consignment to hell.

(For these and other details about the afterlife, see my book, *The Faith Once for All*, chapter 29 on "The Intermediate State.")

IS CREMATION MORALLY PERMISSIBLE?

QUESTION: Is it wrong to cremate the body of a deceased person? Does this practice in some way violate the Christian belief in the resurrection of the dead?

ANSWER: I have a book called "The History of American Funeral Directing," written by Robert Habenstein and William Lamers (1955). On page 4 the authors point out the cultural diversity regarding the choice of methods of disposing of bodies:

> Assume that we are confronted with the dead body of a man. What disposition shall we make of it? Shall we lay it in a boat that is set adrift? Shall we take the heart from it and bury it in one place and the rest of the body in another? Shall we expose it to wild animals? Burn it on a pyre? Push it into a pit naked to rot with other bodies? Boil it until the flesh falls off the bones, and throw the flesh away and treasure the bones? Such questions provoke others which may not even be consciously articulated, such as: "What do men generally think this body is?" And, "What do they think is a proper way of dealing with it?"

The customs mentioned above, plus many others, have been used throughout the history of mankind. The Biblical data show that in Bible times and among Bible people, the most common method of dealing with dead bodies was through some form of burial. Since there is no biblically recorded divine command to do this, we conclude that burial was a matter of custom rather than command. Burial of the dead was the practice of most of the pagan cultures mentioned in the Bible as well. ("Unger's Bible Dictionary" [1978], pp. 158-159, explains the Egyptian, Babylonian, and Philistine customs. Habenstein and Lamers explain the Egyptian, Greek, and Roman practices, pp. 7-46).

In the Old Testament there are few references to the burning of dead bodies. In Leviticus 20:14 and 21:9 "burning" was the penalty for certain serious sins (see Genesis 38:24). Unless this refers to the death penalty by burning, it must refer to the cremation of the remains of one who has been stoned to death for such sins (see Deuteronomy 22:21; John 8:5). We should not infer from this, however, that such cremation was regarded as inherently wrong or always negative. In 1 Samuel 31:12 the bodies of King Saul and his sons, subjected to humiliation by victorious Philistines, were rescued by certain Israelites and reverently burned.

In the New Testament there are many references to tombs and burial, most notably to the burial of the dead body of Jesus Himself in the tomb of Joseph of Arimathea. We can make a strong case for the fact that God's plan to raise Jesus from the dead required burial as the only compatible way to "dispose" of His body following the crucifixion. That Jesus lived and died in a culture that practiced burial was thus a part of God's providential preparation for Jesus's resurrection. This does not mean that burial is the only such method approved by God, any more than Jesus's dying on a cross means that crucifixion is the only method of death approved by God. We must be careful to avoid the "Christological fallacy" of assuming that everything Jesus did puts us under a moral obligation to do the same. Such a fallacy obscures the uniqueness of Jesus's mission.

The main consideration in determining the method of disposing of dead bodies is the fact that human beings are made in the image of God (Genesis 1:26-27). This puts us into a unique category among earthly creatures. Everything about the human race is special when compared and contrasted with the animal kingdom. Human life is not exactly like animal life, nor is human death exactly like animal death. As creatures made in God's image, we should treat ourselves and all other human beings with deep respect.

This applies to all aspects of our nature as human beings, i.e., to both human souls (spirits) and human bodies. Strictly speaking, only our souls are made in God's image, sharing His personhood; but the soul is given a compatible physical form by which to express its godly abilities and characteristics. This means that our bodies must be respected because they are in a sense the divinely-provided and divinely-intended habitations for our souls. (And, for Christians, the body is also the habitation of God the Holy Spirit Himself: 1 Corinthians 6:19-20.)

Thus we must have respect for our bodies while we are alive, and also after we die. We must always treat the bodies of the dead with reverential respect, but it seems to me that burial is not the only way to do this. No matter how careful and elaborate the burial process is, unless there are special circumstances (e.g., freezing or mummification), the dead body will ultimately decay and turn to dust (Genesis 3:19). As I see it, cremation is simply accomplishing the same result, only much faster (among other things).

The questioner, however, raises a specific theological issue: does cremation somehow violate or interfere with our Christian hope of resurrection of the dead on the day of Christ's return? John 5:28-29 says, "An hour is coming, in which all who are in the tombs will hear His voice, and will come forth." Do our dead bodies have to be physically located in their graves (or tombs) in order to experience resurrection?

Without a doubt, our bodies WILL be raised from the dead. We must not assume too much about HOW this will take place, however. We need to remember that the new body will not be the same as the body that died (1 Corinthians 15:36-41), which probably means it will not have the same kind of molecular makeup as our present bodies, much less the very same atoms and molecules. The event of resurrection will not be the restoration and reanimation of rotten corpses and scattered atoms, reconstituted into bodies that burst through the surface of the earth, zombie-like. It will be more in the nature of another act of *ex nihilo* creation, as God gives us not just a new body but also a totally new *kind* of bodily material, adapted to our eternal home (the new heavens and new earth) rather than to this present earthly one. We will simply be "resomafied," or rebodied. (I invented the word "resomafied," from the Greek word for "body," *sōma*.) This is the sense in which our bodies will be "transformed" (Philippians 3:21).

This does not mean we will have a completely different kind of *shape*. Our bodies will be like Christ's glorified body (Philippians 3:21), and when Stephen saw Christ in his new body he readily identified him as the human Jesus (Acts 7:54-60). Thus we have every reason to believe that our new bodies will have the same form as the bodies with which God endowed the human race in the beginning. This implies that in our new bodies we will maintain the same recognizable identities we now possess; hence we will know each other in heaven. We do not know how this applies to infants and children, but we may speculate that the omniscient God will give to those who die young a body comparable to what their matured earthly bodies would have been.

The bottom line is that the resurrection of the dead does not depend upon the postmortem preservation of this present body in any form. Once we die, we are in reality finished with this body. We may be emotionally attached to the bodies and burial places of loved ones, but those bodies are no longer theologically significant. The souls (spirits) of the dead are what continue to exist; we are in some sense in their presence (Hebrews 12:1) no matter where we are upon the face of this earth, and regardless of what has happened to their bodies.

My judgment is that there is nothing wrong with the practice of cremation as a way of disposing of the body of anyone who dies.

ABOUT THE AUTHOR*

(Photo collage – left to right/top to bottom)

1. Jack Cottrell teaching CBS freshman English at 7 a.m., Tuesday through Friday, for three years (1959-1962). This was his first teaching gig.

2. Dr. Cottrell received his Master of Divinity from Westminster Theological Seminary in 1965.

3. The Cottrells (Jack, Barbara, Russell, Cathleen and Susan), circa 1980.

4. Young Jackie was licking his shoelace in an effort to lace his shoe. Quite advanced for a 3 or 4 year old! Also pictured, "Tootsie", his much-loved doll.

5. Dr. Cottrell knows who is the REAL superhero! (This is his favorite T-shirt!)

6. "My first year of full-time teaching at CBS was 1967-1968. This was also the year the new Library-Graduate School building was completed. Here we are moving books from the old third-floor library in Old Main to the new library."

---

*Photograph descriptions provided by Cathleen Cottrell with quotes from Dr. Cottrell.

THE COLLECTED WRITINGS
OF JACK COTTRELL
(Published to Date)

- The Unity of Truth - Vol. 1
- God's Word is Truth - Vol. 2
- The God of the Bible - Vol. 3
- The Bible Versus Calvinism - Vol. 4
- One Baptism Into Christ - Vol. 5
- Biblical Anthropology: Man, Sin, and Death - Vol. 6

Watch for additional volumes coming soon!

Made in the USA
Lexington, KY
27 March 2019